Palgrave Texts in Counselling

Series Editors
Arlene Vetere
Family Therapy and Systemic Practice
VID Specialized University
Oslo, Norway

Rudi Dallos
Clinical Psychology
Plymouth University
Plymouth, UK

This series introduces readers to the theory and practice of counselling and psychotherapy across a wide range of topical issues. Ideal for both trainees and practitioners, the books will appeal to anyone wishing to use counselling and psychotherapeutic skills and will be particularly relevant to workers in health, education, social work and related settings. The books in this series emphasise an integrative orientation weaving together a variety of models including, psychodynamic, attachment, trauma, narrative and systemic ideas. The books are written in an accessible and readable style with a focus on practice. Each text offers theoretical background and guidance for practice, with creative use of clinical examples.

Arlene Vetere, Professor of Family Therapy and Systemic Practice at VID Specialized University, Oslo, Norway.

Rudi Dallos, Emeritus Professor, Dept. of Clinical Psychology, University of Plymouth, UK.

More information about this series at
http://www.palgrave.com/gp/series/16540

Arlene Vetere · Jim Sheehan
Editors

Long Term Systemic Therapy

Individuals, Couples and Families

Editors
Arlene Vetere
Family Therapy and Systemic Practice
VID Specialized University
Oslo, Norway

Jim Sheehan
Family Therapy and Systemic Practice
VID Specialized University
Oslo, Norway

ISSN 2662-9127   ISSN 2662-9135   (electronic)
Palgrave Texts in Counselling and Psychotherapy
ISBN 978-3-030-44510-2   ISBN 978-3-030-44511-9   (eBook)
https://doi.org/10.1007/978-3-030-44511-9

Cover illustration: Akash Raut/EyeEm/gettyimages

This Palgrave Macmillan imprint is published by the registered company Springer Nature Switzerland AG
The registered company address is: Gewerbestrasse 11, 6330 Cham, Switzerland

Foreword

When I was asked to write this Foreword my immediate reaction was to feel unsure about whether or not I knew enough about long term therapy to be able to comment. I then asked what exactly is long term therapy? Is it anything longer than the CBT fixed session protocols or the usual 6 approved insurance sessions? Working in the field of eating disorders this does not even touch the sides.

It seems to me that there are different types of long term therapy: firstly there is the situation where a therapist sees a client for ongoing sessions for a significant length of time; secondly there is the situation where a therapist sees a client at differing points in their lives and thirdly there is the situation where the therapist offers a client an ongoing support over a number of years for a specific reason without necessarily offering sessions. In the field of family therapy I believe these also apply but would include the whole or parts of the family.

I would like to describe 3 such examples of my therapeutic work to demonstrate these ideas.

I have one male client who I first saw 9 years ago for a set 6 sessions in relation to marital difficulties that he and his wife were having. He had a military history and had spent the early part of his adult life conforming to others' expectations of him. He was lacking in insight and ability to take responsibility for his own behaviour and emotions. 9 years down the line he is a sensitive emotionally aware man who has great insight and ability for self-reflection. He attends currently every 4–6 weeks. When I first met him I would never have imagined that I would still be seeing him at all let alone so regularly. I believe that it is the longevity of our relationship together that has allowed him to be able to do the work that he has done that has involved his early relationships with his parents and wider family, the role the military played in shaping his emotional expression, and his sexuality.

I have had a number of clients that I saw as teenagers that made contact as adults for varying reasons, for example, one client who I saw when she was aged 15 years and had a psychiatric diagnosis of anorexia nervosa. She sent me the occasional email over the years letting me know what she was doing. Then following the birth of her first daughter, when she was in her early thirties, some of her childhood issues resurfaced in her parenting of her daughter. She was able to work through relational difficulties she had with her own mother through thinking about herself as a mother.

In another example, I shall describe a client who I saw when she was aged 15 years, who had a psychiatric diagnosis of bulimia and depression. She was struggling with her dream for herself not being what her parents wanted for her, and again, over the years I got the occasional email telling me about how she was achieving her dream despite her family's opposition. Again in her early thirties she had a crisis when her depression overcame her. She took herself into the jungle, consumed surgical alcohol and cut her own throat. It was a miracle she was found. When she came home she made contact and began to rebuild her life, which ultimately resulted in her developing a new found spirituality and new career path. In addition to this she dealt with the death of her much beloved grandmother, who had been her main source of support within the family, and ran the London Marathon.

The last client I would like to tell you about is a family I first saw 8 years ago when the parents first divorced. There were 2 children, a boy of 8 years and a daughter of 11 years. The boy still wanted to see his Dad but the daughter had found a sexually explicit message from his girlfriend on his phone and withdrawn completely from him, with the support of the mother. My task had been to try to re-engage the father and daughter. The mother eventually moved forward emotionally and actively worked on supporting her daughter re-engaging with her ex-husband although at this point the daughter was adamantly refusing all contact. Despite all our efforts nothing changed. My final intervention was to encourage the father to maintain a level of communication with the daughter that he could sustain without getting anything back. With the mother's support he began telephoning once a week to talk to her, initially this was on the house phone and eventually it was on the brothers' phone. Over the years he called from time to time to talk and up date me on the no change; these conversations, for me, were soul destroying as I felt I had let him down. For 7 years he maintained this until the daughter went to university at which point he said to his daughter if she wanted him to continue talking to her she would need to give him her number. She gave him her number and suggested they text: this was the first time he had got anything back from her. For the last year they have been engaging in text conversations. 2 weeks ago the brother was having a pre prom gathering at home and wanted his Dad there. The father accepted but cautioned that he did not want to make his daughter feel she could not be there, so he would stay away. Via the mother the father was told that the daughter was ok for him to attend. This was the first time he had seen his daughter in 8 years. She spoke to him and they hugged. When I received his email update I cried.

These examples may not be conventional therapy examples; however the common theme is the strong trusting relationship that was developed between the therapist and client. In the current climate too much emphasis, I believe is placed on protocols and replicating treatment plans that can be rolled out to all regardless of whether or not they are a good fit. The personal and individualised approach that these examples show are not possible now for most clients in public sector services.

I value a book that acknowledges long term therapy and the relationships formed between client and therapist that are crucial to that therapy being successful for those involved. This is particularly important in the field of family therapy where several members of the same family can be seen by the same therapist. On more than one occasion I have been referred to as 'our family's' therapist. This, for me, is the way forward for families in the same way a family might have a family GP or family lawyer, they can also have a family therapist.

Maidenhead, UK   Shelagh Wright
August 2019   Systemic Psychotherapist and
                                                      Accredited Family Mediator

Editors' Introduction

Systemic psychotherapy has long been conceptualised and practiced as brief psychotherapy, in both the public sector and in independent practice. There are many schools of practice within the field of systemic psychotherapy, such as, solution focused, Milan systemic, open dialogue approaches, narrative approaches, strategic and structural approaches, narrative attachment, and so on, and all come under the umbrella of brief therapy. Indeed, the brevity of these approaches formed one central plank through which systemic psychotherapy found its own unique identity against the background of more established psychoanalytic approaches to psychotherapy. Systemic psychotherapy, broadly, has developed a robust and ecologically valid evidence base and is recommended within NICE Guidance, UK, for a range of psychiatric disorders (Carr 2014a, b). It sits alongside the other major models of brief psychotherapy, such as, CBT, CAT, behaviour therapy, EMDR, brief focal psychodynamic psychotherapy, and so on. Typically, the brief therapies take place within an average of 5–20 meetings, unless the work is complicated by trauma processes. However, despite being seen as a brief therapy, in our practice and in our supervision work, we notice that many colleagues offer systemic therapy over the longer term.

Both Jim Sheehan and Arlene Vetere are systemic supervisors. We both supervise experienced systemic psychotherapists and systemic practitioners. Increasingly we notice that our supervisees bring to the supervision their longer term practice. This can take many forms, for example, long term systemic psychotherapy over 3–5 years, and more, perhaps with some managed breaks in the process; working with different generations in a family system over the course of a life cycle, perhaps working with the children, and then with the children as adults, or with their children; or working with different parts of an extended family system at different times; and offering an on-demand service to individuals, couples and families over an extended period of time, including bi-annual 'top up' meetings. Our supervisees bring their dilemmas, their ethical concerns and questions around long term relationships with individuals, family systems, professional teams, supervision groups, and professional-family systems. At the heart of many of their questions is a focus on the extent to which systemic theory can accommodate and formulate long term practice, and where might be the boundaries of the systemic theories that both help to explain and give direction to the work. At what point might a supervisee need to incorporate and integrate other explanatory models into their systemic thinking, and what might this mean for systemic practice? How does the relative longevity of the work impact the way practitioners build and maintain therapeutic relationships with the relational systems they assist? And what implications does such longevity have on, and for, the supervisory needs of systemic psychotherapists at the heart of the work? Given the absence of a rigorous evidence base for long term systemic therapy and practice, how can we and our supervisees hold ourselves ethically accountable for what we do and what we think?

Both of us also work systemically over the longer term, with individual clients, couples and families, and we also offer long term consultation with teams, agencies and organisations. So we too are exercised by the above questions and dilemmas. In editing this book, we have invited experienced systemic psychotherapists who are also experienced supervisors to write about and reflect on their experiences of longer term systemic work, and the implications for systemic theory in their area of practice.

All the contributors are well known in their field and have extensive experience of writing for publication: Ros Draper; Chip Chimera; Ana Aguirregabiria; Helga Hanks; Sarah Houston; T. K. Lang; Paddy Sweeney and Martin Daly. We too both contribute a chapter each.

The book is divided into four parts of working therapeutically with (a) couples and families, (b) with individuals, (c) with professional practitioner groups and (d) with family businesses. In preparing our chapters, some authors have invited their clients, with whom they have worked together over the longer term to contribute some thoughts about their experiences of being in such a long lived relationship, for example, the chapters by Chip Chimera, Ros Draper and Arlene Vetere.

We shall briefly introduce each chapter in relation to how systemic theory is used to understand the relational processes involved in longer term systemic psychotherapy. Jim Sheehan writes about his work with couples where one of them is challenged by a lengthy chronic illness. Systemic theory illuminates the impact of the illness on the person, their partner, their relationship and their family/social support systems and how their circumstances and wider relational contexts influence the progression of the illness. In working with couples over the longer term, Jim explores how expected and unexpected life events, and the life cycle changes for the couple and their relationship all benefit from an ongoing therapeutic relationship where trust and commitment enable either frequent or infrequent consultation and therapy as needed. In her chapter on working with couples and families, Arlene explores how some people simply need longer to process and resolve unresolved hurts and losses in their relationships. A typical couple therapy might consist of 10–20 meetings, but for some, as Arlene shows, more time is needed to consolidate and make coherent the systemic experiences of healing, forgiveness and repair. The development of a shared narrative as to how and why the therapy was helpful often depends on the integration of, and reflection on, all aspects of intimate experiences and this where the passage of time affords the opportunity.

There are 3 chapters on working systemically with individuals. Both Ros and Chip draw on their clients' reflections—in Ros' chapter to construct the account, and in Chip's to weave together her reflections with that of her client's. Chip writes of her therapeutic relationship with her client and their joint challenge to identify and resolve early adaptive self-protective processes of dissociation, and other unresolved trauma responses to relational danger, that in adulthood get in the way of developing trusting and intimate relationships. Ros, in her chapter, uses a relationally discursive approach to co-construct accounts of the development and progression of the therapeutic relationship and therapeutic changes over time. Neither Ros nor Chip shy away from addressing the challenges of longer term systemic work with individuals and focus on processes of healing and repair in the therapeutic alliance. Sarah works systemically with young people, and although the length of time spent in the work might be relatively shorter than, say with the adult-focused work discussed by Chip and Ros in their chapters, nevertheless, Sarah uses systemic theory to show how subjective time and distressing experience can seem extended during adolescence, and thus how to assist young people in navigating bumps in the road of their emotional and relational development.

There are three chapters on extended group supervision with professional practitioners. This partly addresses a clear gap in the systemic literature (Henning 2016) and also offers an opportunity for all four authors to explore what is enabled by the length of time afforded the group members. Helga writes of how a committed supervision relationship with peers and supervisors in a group setting enables the development of interpersonal trust such that deeper recesses of experience can be accessed and processed in the group with the group members. Her emphasis on self care and care of others in extremely challenging working contexts shows us all how persistence and emphasis on small acts of care and kindness can systemically reverberate throughout the wider working system. Similarly TK and Paddy and Martin in their systemic group work with pastoral care teams and health care providers explore and illuminate the development of processes of trust and trusting behaviour that enables and sustains professional receptivity and complex emotional risk-taking in their day-to-day work. All three chapters explore the parallel processes and emotional dynamics in group work that can mirror similar processes in the workplace and in other walks of life.

Finally, Ana in her chapter on working systemically with family businesses illustrates the complex interplay and weave of family life and family relationships with business roles, business hierarchies and working relationships. Such interplay can lead to emotional dilemmas and discrepancies that are harder to resolve, such as the reversal of hierarchies, power and influence across the two domains of work and family, conflicts of loyalty between family and business roles, and the attachment dilemmas at the heart of such complexity.

We hope this book will begin a process of addressing this huge gap in the systemic literature between long term systemic practice on the ground and a lack of theorising and research around longer term systemic work. We want this book to both be a resource for practitioners and supervisors, and to celebrate a growing interest in theory-practice linking in long term systemic psychotherapy.

August 2019   Arlene Vetere
                                                     Jim Sheehan

References

Carr, A. (2014a). The evidence base for family therapy and systemic interventions with child-focused problems. *Journal of Family Therapy, 36*, 107–157.

Carr, A. (2014b). The evidence base for couple therapy, family therapy and systemic interventions with adult-focused problems. *Journal of Family Therapy, 36*, 158–194.

Henning, M. (2016). *Positive dynamics: A systemic narrative approach to facilitating groups.* London: Palgrave Macmillan.

Contents

Notes on Contributors

Ana Aguirregabiria is a reliable and effective family therapist and clinical psychologist. Ana has over two decades of experience in working with families, improving their relationships and bringing greater understanding and meaning to their interactions. Ana has a grounded commitment to provide the best support to her clients by continuing her own learning and development. She is a registered clinical psychologist (HCPC), chartered clinical psychologist and Associate Fellow of the British Psychological Society. She started working in the NHS a a clinical psychologist and a few years later started her own independent practice where she works full time.

Dr. Chip Chimera is a systemic family therapist and psychodrama psychotherapist with a special interest in the Dynamic Maturational Model of attachment. She is the Director for Continuing Professional Development and Innovation at the Institute of Family Therapy, London. Chip has a particular interest in how family therapists integrate action methods into their work which was the subject of her doctoral studies. She works in independent practice with a range of individuals, families and groups.

In recent years she has also specialised in working with trauma organised systems, particularly those families who have engaged in prolonged custody disputes.

Martin Daly is also a Catholic priest, family therapist and systemic practitioner. He trained at the Mater Hospital Family Therapy Training Programme. Until recently he has been Principal at a large Dublin secondary school. He has a particular interest in systems based leadership in educational and other settings and has completed doctoral studies in Leadership and Management. He practices as a family therapist and as a consultant to groups and organisations.

Ros Draper is a systemic psychotherapist, supervisor and consultant with many years experience working in the public sector and in private practice. With David Campbell, Ros co-founded the influential Systemic Thinking and Practice book series and has co-authored with Rudi Dallos *An Introduction to Family Therapy* now in its 4th edition. Ros is passionate about the usefulness of systemic ideas and the distinctive difference these ideas make to the practice of psychotherapy.

Helga Hanks practiced as a Consultant Clinical Psychologist, Analytic Psychotherapist and Systemic Family Therapist, in St James's University Hospital, Leeds. Until her retirement from her fulltime post she was also a Visiting Senior Lecturer at the Institute of Psychological Sciences, Leeds University. She is one of the founder members of the Leeds Family Therapy & Research Centre (LFTRC) at Leeds University which came into existence in 1979. She has been Clinical Director of the Centre until 2005. She is one of the core staff who developed the M.Sc. in Systemic Family Therapy at the Institute of Psychological Sciences, Leeds University. Since 2001 she has worked in the Community Paediatric Department, Leeds Community Healthcare NHS Trust. There she worked with NHS staff supporting them emotionally and psychologically. Since 1980 she has provided systemic training and supervision for a wide variety of professionals. She retired in 2019. The *Journal of Human Systems* was first published in 1990 and she was a founder Member of that Journal. She continues to be on the Editorial Board and has since 2017 been joint editor of the Journal. She has published and researched widely both in the areas of family therapy and child abuse.

Sarah Houston is systemic psychotherapist working in Childrens' Health Ireland at Our Lady's Children's Hospital Crumlin, in Dublin. She works in a specialist therapy service for children and adolescents who have experienced sexual abuse, and their families. She also works in private practice as a systemic psychotherapist and supervisor. She has a background in social work and has been working in the area of mental health for 20 years, much of which has involved working with children, young people and families in Child and Adolescent Mental Health Services. She has many years' experience teaching on social work and family therapy programmes at undergraduate and masters level. She lives in Dublin.

T. K. Lang, Dr. Theol. is Associate Professor in Theology at The University of Oslo. He works as Family Therapist and Supervisor, and has for more than 35 years been supervisor for ministers, family therapists, social workers, physicians, and other professionals. For many years one of the editors of "Omsorg: Nordisk tidsskrift for Palliativ Medisin" (Nordic Journal of *Palliative Medicine*). He is the co-author of *Der fremtiden blir til: Et dialogisk paradigme for veiledning* (*Where the Future is Formed: A Dialogic Paradigme for Supervision*). He has been in private practice as a family therapist since 1989.

Jim Sheehan, Ph.D. is professor of family therapy and systemic practice at VID Specialized University, Oslo. He is a social worker, systemic psychotherapist and systemic supervisor, practising and resident in Ireland. With Arlene Vetere he co-edited *Supervision of Family Therapy and Systemic Practice* for Springer, 2018.

Paddy Sweeney is a Catholic priest, a family therapist and systemic practitioner. Trained at the Mater Hospital, Family Therapy Training Programme in Dublin and at the Tavistock Clinic in London he currently holds responsibility for the well being of clergy and church workers in Dublin. This responsibility is enacted through one to one work with individuals, the Ministering Reflectively programme, consulting to groups and offering training.

Arlene Vetere, Ph.D. is professor of family therapy and systemic practice at VID Specialized University, Oslo. She is a clinical psychologist, systemic psychotherapist and systemic supervisor, registered and resident in the UK. Arlene and Jim Sheehan co-edited *Supervision of Family Therapy and Systemic Practice* for Springer, 2018.

List of Figures

Part I

Long Term Systemic Work with Couples and Families

1

Couple and Family Therapy as Meta-Theory: Doing Relational Therapy in the Longer Term

Arlene Vetere

Some families and couples come back. Some never want to leave. Some want a longer term relationship and some want regular top-ups over a number of years. This is not unhelpful dependency, rather it is a sophisticated reckoning of how autonomy and dependency are different sides (aspects) of inter-personal trust. It is in the longer term that relationships of more deeply felt trust can emerge, and it is in this realm of deeper trust that more is possible. In the short term of course, much can happen in effective systemic couple and family therapy to improve emotional life: for example, family members address and heal unresolved hurt and loss; they develop their capacity for comforting, interactive arousal regulation and self-soothing; they shift from traumatic states of mind to an integration of thought, feeling, action and intention expressed as more coherent communication of wants and needs—thus leading to more effective problem solving; and they develop their capacities for play and reflective curiosity about the states of mind of others. But some of us cannot

A. Vetere (✉)
Family Therapy and Systemic Practice, VID Specialized University, Oslo, Norway

© The Author(s) 2020
A. Vetere and J. Sheehan (eds.), *Long Term Systemic Therapy*,
Palgrave Texts in Counselling and Psychotherapy,
https://doi.org/10.1007/978-3-030-44511-9_1

3

achieve this level of change in the shorter term. Some of us simply need longer.

In this chapter, I shall explore some of the reasons why relational change might need to occur at a slower pace, the nature of the emotional danger and risks experienced in the therapeutic work, and the resolution of traumatic states of mind. For example, beliefs about oneself and others can become rigid and unyielding in traumatic states. This is because they are reinforced both through a lack of an effective challenge to these beliefs and also, paradoxically, through unsuccessful attempts not to repeat in the future and for the next generation what was experienced as unhelpful in earlier life. The understanding of the rigid application of corrective and replicative scripts in family life will be at the heart of this chapter. Importantly, I have asked two families to contribute their thoughts about their experiences of longer term systemic therapeutic work. Their participation and reflections will underline the need for research into the efficacy and effectiveness of longer term systemic psychotherapy with couples and families.

The Emergence of Systemic Family Therapy

Systemic couple and family therapy emerged and evolved in the second half of the twentieth century in response to therapeutic requests for relational change. Individual therapeutic work, whilst effective, sometimes met insurmountable challenges in the push for individual change, such as the unbalancing of complementary power relationships, resulting in family members striving for a return to a more known and predictable status quo, and/or a relational context that could neither welcome nor support individual change. Unacknowledged fears and anxieties about the impact of individual change on family members' relationships simply got in the way of desired progress. Thus was systemic therapy born—in the attempt to work with social and emotional relationships and contexts to support the emergence of change in the face of both non-conscious and conscious fears and anxieties about the meaning and impact of difference. Thus theory developed to explain and formulate in practice why change is feared; and how oppressive contexts can make desired change difficult e.g. economic and social exclusion, the experience of not belonging, a lack of social support, and so on. Although systemic therapy was positioned in practice as short term in relation to the dominance of psychoanalytic and behavioural approaches at the time, theoretically it always recognised change was a continual, dynamic process mediated by the need for some stability and predictability in relationships i.e. according to how we manage and cope, individually and relationally, with life cycle events, both expected and unexpected, and with our family and social circumstances. This leaves the theoretical door open for the recognition of the challenges of change and for the unspoken, unsayable and often different needs, hopes and desires of family members, and thus why, in some instances, and for some couples and families, overt change might need to take longer.

The Inter-Related Levels of Change

Change is formulated in systemic practice at four levels: (a) behavioural change—a recognition that repeated sequences of interaction become patterned, habitual and taken-for-granted, such that curiosity is not brought into play about how these patterns developed, or what maintains them; (b) cognitive change—the beliefs, ideas, values and meanings held at a group level that underpin family members' intentions and behaviours with one another; (c) emotional change—the history of attachments in the family system, the development of empathic attunement and reflexivity in relationships, safety and protection, comforting and soothing, interactive regulation of arousal, unresolved hurt and loss, and so on and (d) contextual change—exploring and illuminating the social. economic and political discourses, events and circumstances that can both facilitate and hinder change and development, and working with networks of social support in family, professional and community sytems to promote wellbeing for all. Systemic theory integrates and formulates information across all four levels of change whilst encouraging a "helicopter view" of family circumstances with a constant focus on the relationship between content and process in our everyday interactions. The development of a compassionate and non-reactive "observing position" in relation to our-selves, our loved ones, and our challenges, dilemmas and resources and opportunities for change is the hallmark of systemic therapy, both in the short and longer term.

Many of the pioneer systemic family therapists were originally psy-chodynamically or psychoanalytically trained. For example, Minuchin worked in Israel as a child psychotherapist with children of the holo-caust before moving to the USA and working to empower young, black, impoverished mothers and their wayward sons. In another example, the early Milan team developed their approach to systemic therapy in the context of slow, regular monthly meetings with their careful, cool work with families with long standing developmental difficulties i.e. eating dis-orders that emerge in adolescence and continued voraciously into adult-hood, and long term experiences with psychosis. In both these examples, there was a recognition that for some families, and for some entrenched difficulties, there was a need to pace the work differently.

Inter-Generational Patterns of Attachment: Looking Up and Down the Generations

How do we look forward into the future? And how do we look into the past? Where do we see influence and legacies of developmental experi-ences, and on what are our hopes for a preferred future based? When we work therapeutically with parents and children, and couples, of any age, asking questions about the relationship between the respective grand–parents' relationships can bring out stories about the parents' childhood experiences and thus prompt a consideration of how their own chil-dren experience their relationship as a mother and/or a father. For exam-ple, we might ask parents or partners: How would you describe your parents' relationship—cool, warm, distant, passionate, loyal, any con-flicts/conflict resolution and so on? What differences do you see, if any, in the relationships between your mother's parents versus your father's par-ents? In what ways are either of your parents' relationships similar to your own? The resulting reflections open a discussion of inter-generational corrective and replicative scripts i.e. those practices of care giving and care receiving in close relationships that we intentionally try to repeat, or to change for the next generation as parents in our turn, or for ourselves and our partners. The conversation can then explore these intentions and their perceived impacts and outcomes in family life: for example, What have you tried to make similar or different to either of these relationships? What do you value versus feel critical about in either of your parents' relationships? However, therein lies a paradox—we are often trying to make better an aspect of care giving and care receiving for which we hold no workable mental representation ourselves. If it was not done for us, if we were not comforted and held, for example, we might not know well how to do it, what it feels like and looks like, and so on. It may take time to learn—to develop new neural pathways and behavioural patterns.

We explore the influence of these inter-generational patterns on the parents' relationship with their own children—we ask questions that invite the parents to consider how their own experiences have consciously or non-consciously influenced and shaped their relationships with their children: How do you see your relationship (mother and father in turn) with your children? How are you different with your children to how your parents were with you? Do you think you are closer or more distant to your children than your parents were with you? What do you hope your children will learn from you for the benefit of their future relationships? As we walk around in the recollections and sense memories that are stimulated in these conversational moments, we can invite partners and family members to listen whilst one is speaking, and/or we can encourage a dialogue. Such conversations can be poignant, and often need to proceed slowly and gently, or they can be touched on in a regular way during the meetings. Either way, we are trying to create safe spaces where family members can order and re-order their experiences, without fear of censure. It is in our constant validation of their intentions to make things better for their relationships and for the next generation that inter-personal trust deepens.

Patterns of Inter-Generational Trauma in Families

The experience of inter-generational trauma in families can lead to rigidity in responding, despite positive intentions to make things better. In the face of relational danger, when the need for safety and protection is high, family members might become emotionally overwhelmed which can lead to chaotic behavioural responding and too much unpredictability in parents' availability, on the one hand, and on the other hand, it can lead to increasingly escalating and rigid attempts to protect and be safe through the repetition of solutions that do not work. The irony lies in family members knowing that their rigid attempts to control safety and manage fear do not work, yet not knowing what else to do. People can often articulate this dilemma with frustration, distress and despair. At the heart of both these patterns of responding i.e. chaotic and unpredictable attempts to maintain safety, and the rigid application of a "narrow" solution, lies the intention to make things better and to do things better than in previous generations. And herein lies the rub, unprocessed trauma experiences and responding constrain the integration of experience and the development of reflective functioning in the context of those experiences. Family members are like pioneers in these moments. They do not hold mental representations of what better looks like, feels like, or does like. They simply know they want matters to be better—and sorely feel the disappointment when this appears not to happen. Courage and resilience become overshadowed in the developing story of how we have failed as a family, failed as parents, or how others have failed us. Although part of the therapeutic task is to help family members own their experiences of courage and resilience, deeply embedded feelings of shame and unspoken feelings of inadequacy get in the way. Thus, for some people, these feelings take time to emerge, to be heard, to be explored, to be ordered and re-ordered, and to be processed and resolved, with patience, gentleness and commitment by all.

In our therapeutic work we may meet families with emotional cut-offs, and rifts and feuds across generations, with the original reasons long forgotten. Secrets in families can exist where family members are not able, willing or prepared to face the costs of revealing the secret, for example, childhood sexual abuse, domestic violence, bankruptcy, public shaming in an earlier generation, and so on. For example, when we experience a tension between who we are told we are versus who we feel ourselves to be, we may try to hide from others' gaze. Nothing is as it seems. We can experience a state of unresolvable confusion when asked to choose between belonging or autonomy. The feelings of shame are an uncomfortable signal of this tension. Many of us are most vulnerable to feeling shame and being shamed by those we love and wish to be close to, and find acceptance. If our protest at feeling this dilemma comes to naught we may become helpless and silenced and these are the circumstances under which we can develop a "false self" i.e. presenting the world with what we think others want to see. The dilemma of shame is stark i.e. how do we maintain an authentic self awareness in the face of a parent's or partner's disapproval, with the risk of losing valuable support, versus trying to be what others want, with the resulting loss of autonomy. If we work therapeutically with family members who shame and belittle others it presents a challenge to the processes of engagement and the development of inter-personal trust in the therapeutic alliance. In trying to maintain a position of curiosity, we ask, what happened to you? Persistence and perseverance in the face of shame and shaming, touched with kindness, leads to a recognition of the mutual lack of entitlement to be heard, and to have our needs responded to as we hope.

In the safety of a therapeutic relationship we can explore how certain emotions and emotional states have become feared and avoided, at all costs, in an effort to self-protect, for example, how patterns of self-protection learned in childhood to survive adversity, and sometimes cruelty, go past their "sell by date" in adulthood and lead to problems in trusting others, and to establishing and maintaining intimacy. Family members may have learned that emotions are not a good guide to action because they did not get them what they needed as a child, for example, affirmation, comfort, reassurance—being seen, heard and known in our own right. Alternately, being raised in a family context of high and unregulated emotional/physiological arousal, with or without the fear of physical violence where no one was able to help them make meaning, to understand emotion, to regulate arousal and learn self-control, leaves family members quickly triggered by signs of conflict and hostility. Experiencing constant states of high arousal leaves little room for thought, let alone reflective thought, as they seem always to be in a state of "fight/flight". This impacts on the developing ability to learn how to trust, to learn to calm down, when perhaps psychoactive substances have substituted for self-regulation. If emotional numbing and dissociation have emerged as the dominant self-protective strategy, self harm and psychoactive substances may be used to feel alive—to get back into their bodies! But the idea that such fearful and shameful memories can be confronted and resolved can be terrifying, if not at times, horrifying. Relationships can, in many ways be both the cause of, and solution to, our difficulties at one and the same time. For example, the very person who has the power to hold me and comfort me, to keep me safe and warm, is also the person who can frighten me, reject me and even abandon me. Unresolvable dilemmas in our close relationships can drive us mad. When there is no one to help us understand and illuminate these dilemmas, to develop a reflective meaningful view of what is happening to us, and to the others around us, we have very little choice. Chip Chimera, in her chapter, writes about the impact on children's development of long term hostility between separated and divorced parents and the unwillingness of one or both to address and resolve the loyalty binds that capture their children. Longer term relational therapy is often required to help parents move to a position of wishing to resolve their "implacable hatred" such that their child/ren do not have to resolve the resulting loyalty binds by swearing allegiance to one parent over another. Reflection and reflexivity in some aspects of our relational functioning can sometimes take a long time to develop, and needs patient and persistent work in the face of continuous disappointment.

Inter-Personal Trust in Long Term Systemic Psychotherapy

Chris and his wife Jacqui, have been working with me in long term systemic couple therapy. Let us hear Chris' account of why he needed the time, and how he used the longer time frame to both trust the process and to process his own and their relational experiences.

Jacqui and I have known each other for over 35 years and have been married for 32 of them. Some of these years have been challenging in the way we communicated (or a better way of putting it is, sometimes didn't), and so we had several attempts at various "couples counselling" sessions. All of these were short time frame (months) and limited in number of sessions and as such I found them very intense and I came away with the impression of them being a tick-box approach—a set list of things/questions/techniques they wanted to cover in the time allowed. I did not find these sessions very helpful as they just didn't work for me!

I also have several challenges—I am a logical "if there's a problem then let's go-do / fix it type of person" which is not always helpful in a relationship issue, and I am very unlikely to (read, won't) talk to somebody I don't know (and by my nature, hence don't actually trust), especially about anything as personal as my relationship with my wife. So, the key for me was a long term (several years) approach, with no real agenda or list of things to cover (well if there was it didn't feel like it).

Arlene was a great find—we worked with her over several years (I think over 5) on a weekly basis initially, and then as time went on these were extended to monthly and then every 2–3 months until when we decided we had reached a stage when we could stop.

This slow extended pace worked perfectly for me as it allowed me to:

- *Digest things at my pace (I have to think about stuff like this a lot before it sinks in and I can balance it with the Mr fix-it me, as compared to my other half, J, who gets it extremely quickly).*
- *Build a relationship with (which for me brings a level of trust) with the counsellor/process and so actually be able to talk about stuff.*
- *As we learned how to manage the times of mis-communication better, it was essential for me to be able to come back and go through any "events" again to see where I missed any cues and could learn from them.*

We still have times of mis-communication, but we can handle them a lot, lot better—the extended period of time with Arlene was very well spent!

When we work therapeutically with those who were exposed to unpro-
tected and uncomforted relational danger as children, we often use the
past to validate the present—"you needed to survive in the way you did,
but now this seems to trip you up, and makes intimacy and close connection harder to achieve." In the work, we affirm our clients' safety strategies, and recognise that sometimes we withdraw for fear of making things
worse. This is how some of us have learned to keep ourselves safe. Such
recognition of the intention behind the withdrawal in a difficult inter-
personal moment, paves the way for clients to be courageous and to take
emotional risks with those they love. We help people play with ideas and
try them on for size, for example, see whether this can help you, perhaps
take action and then ask, do you perceive/experience things differently?
As practitioners we stay with the process, for as long as it takes for people
to feel sufficiently secure with us, and thus with their family members.
Based in his research, Van der Kolk (2014) argues that the best predictor
of what happens after exposure to frightening, dangerous experiences and
events is whether and to what extent a person can seek and take comfort,
not the trauma history itself. As Dan Siegel and Marion Solomon (2003)
write, "It's bearable because it's shareable." For example, we might ask,
who held and comforted you? If there was someone, we might then ask,
what would they say now? If there was no one, we might ask, tell me how
you survive now. With relational trauma, the "other" is both the source
of and the solution to our fear. This is what makes it so complex and
so frightening for some people to learn to trust again, and what holds
them in a rigid if not "frozen" state of mind. If this fear is complicated
by shame—both feeling and believing that "I am the mistake", rather
than that "I have made a mistake", it requires adequate time to process,
re-order and resolve experiences of loss, humiliation and betrayal.

John Gottman (2011) considers that the "perpetual" relational issues
in our lives that defy easy resolution always have powerful attachment
significance. In Gottman's work with couples where one feels betrayed
and abandoned by the other's "affair" i.e. when one partner turns outside
the relationship for sex/affection/comfort/connection, and so on, and the
couple wish to remake their relationship, he argues that the process of

acknowledgement, apology and reconciliation needs to take as long as it needs to take. And this could be a very long time. Then can the process of understanding what happened in the marriage begin in a more focused way, such that a "new" relationship is forged. Resolution of the felt experience of loss and betrayal requires that their partner becomes predictable again: a reciprocal process of accessibility and responsiveness. This means that future moments of mis-attunement can be acknowledged, talked about, apologised for, and healed. This is the kind of forgiveness that enables emotional risk-taking in relationships and thus why, for some, it takes a long time. But how does apology work? To take in an apology and to believe its healing intention, we need to see from the other's behaviour that they have been affected by our hurt and care about that—but what if we have learned from childhood experience not to read faces, as facial expression signalled danger? Does this mean we cannot see a look of concern on the other's face, so we cannot conceive of the positive intention not to hurt us and the wish to heal? As Susan Johnson (2002) writes in her Emotion Focussed Therapy, attachment injuries, or moments when we experience the other as not being there for us, letting us down and disappointing us in our heightened moment of need, are not generalised hurts—they define the emotional connection between partners, and between parents and children, as insecure. A felt lack of security in our close relationships leads to separation distress, across the family life cycle. The indelible imprint of relational trauma gets in the way of trusting and healing, and if the partner or parent either minimises or dismisses the hurt, it reconfirms the injury and the belief that "I was right not to trust you – you are not there for me – and you can never be there for me!".

Cultural discourses and mores might influence and shape family members' range of responses to emotionally threatening inter-personal moments, but if we focus on helping family members create a secure base, they can better deal with what their culture asks of them. An attitude of openness in therapy helps us all use familiar ideas in unfamiliar places.

First, We Attend to the Current Dilemmas, and then, the Trauma Stories

Usually, when we meet a couple or a family, they are seeking assistance with current dilemmas and difficulties. And usually, this is where we begin. And often, this is sufficient. We do not always have to explore and connect past dilemmas and hurts with current difficulties in order to illuminate and process those difficulties. But sometimes this is essential. For example, trauma responses can "sleep" and lie dormant and then be triggered by predictable and desirable life cycle events e.g. a child sexually abused might partially resolve some of their trauma responses in adolescence, only to have them re-triggered when planning/becoming pregnant, for fear of not being able to protect their child as they were not protected…

Let us think now about Sonia and her parents. Initially, she asked for help in negotiating with her parents the kind of support she best needed when feeling suicidal and plunging into a state of depression. Her parents were willing participants, and after two to three years of gentle negotiating and following the feedback, they all found a sense of balance in their current relationships that worked for them. And this then paved the way to look back and seek to resolve the unprocessed losses and hurts, for all of them.

Sonia—she is grieving for what is lost. The process of grief is embodied, relational, representational, and developmental. Sonia is now 36 years old. Since the age of 18, she has struggled with the experience of depression and wanting to die. She believes, with a fierce belief, that she is the cause of family difficulties and that she is a bad person. For the past 10 years she has been working with a kind, gentle and determined psychotherapist—determined to help her challenge her unhelpful beliefs about herself. For the past 4 years, she has been working with me, and both her parents. Her mother and father are living together in an unhappy and unsatisfactory marriage that holds a history of unresolved conflict and hurt. Sonia is trying to understand the processes of triangulation in her family. How did she get caught up in her parents' distress and conflict and come to believe it was her responsibility to protect her mother? Her mother has always complained to Sonia about her father.

Now, Sonia wants to de-centralise from their unresolved marital conflict, and wants to keep a loving relationship with her mother and to develop her relationship with her father. When marital discord is associated with family secrecy, children are likely to blame themselves. They feel responsible and develop a sense of guilt towards the parent/s who is hurt. This creates a powerful and confusing mix of unresolved feelings. The expression of anger becomes associated with danger. As Sonia grows up, this interacts with her development of causal understanding in relationships and results in this sense that it is all her fault. She is the bad one. This is reinforced during adolescence and early adulthood by her confused expressions of distress, for example, running away, harming herself and trying to kill herself. These actions cause confusion, pain and hurt for her parents, which further reinforces Sonia's guilt and shame. At some point, her protests do not work, and she falls back into a position of hopelessness and helplessness, diagnosed as severe depression. Sonia believes she has a chemical imbalance in her brain. Sometimes an explanation can be helpful. Recognition and relief can follow, sometimes. Sonia feels alone with her burden. She has two married siblings with children. In talking with our adult siblings, we may find that they made a contribution as well, and took on different patterns of protection. At the time of writing, Sonia's two siblings do not want to join in with the family meetings, nor do they wish for an individual meeting. Sonia can now ask her parents why they stayed together, and would it not have been better had they parted when Sonia and her siblings were younger. Sonia's mother holds a strong corrective script. She wanted to keep her family together at all costs. Why?...Because her own family of origin experience was disconnected, with emotional neglect, emotional cut-offs and lack of coherence. Many, many years later, Sonia's mother reconnected with a sibling and they were both surprised and delighted to discover they could make a strong bond. This sibling died recently, sadly, but perhaps Sonia's mother can see in a different way that relationships can change and evolve?

Here is what Sonia's father, Dinesh, has to say from his experience of long term systemic therapy:

My main observation is that psychotherapy does not offer a fast route to solving long term issues. Understandably, there is an element of repetition in our discussions that involves going over the same ground albeit from a different angle. This created some frustration that needed to be discussed and understood by all. Consequently, it has required a high degree of patience from some of us.

Notwithstanding the frustration, I have learnt a lot through careful analysis of difficult issues. Perhaps, we would have benefited more by having discussions within the family in between our meetings with the therapists. This could potentially reduce our reliance on the therapist as well as making the therapy sessions more productive. However, I do appreciate that this can be difficult unless all participants feel safe in speaking openly.

I have also questioned the definition of long term therapy in the sense that whether therapy spread over a long period has made us complacent and not sufficiently focussed. The fact that you (Arlene) regularly have a status review is a big plus (although I don't believe we as a family make the best use of the status reviews) but I do wonder, for instance, about the time Sonia has been seeing her individual therapist and whether those sessions have become no more than, important though this may be, a comfort blanket for Sonia.

Whilst difficult, it may be helpful if there were any measures of success that could help the participants. For instance, once it has been established that a subject is safe to discuss, the participants could be asked to discuss it at home and report back at a future therapy session, a bit of homework. It would also be helpful if there was a rule of thumb indicating the length of time between therapy sessions. As you can see, my inputs tend to focus more on the practical side rather than the emotional one. Nonetheless, Arlene, I trust this is of some help.

As Dinesh points out, and cautions us, we must seek to ensure a longer term relationship does not lose its way. We may indeed follow some side tracks from time to time, but it is important that all our forays into acknowledgement, understanding, illumination and processing of separate and shared experience have a conjoint focus and a healing purpose.

Now, let us hear what Sonia's mother, Elsa, has to say about her experience of long term systemic therapy.

Our daughter has been suffering mental ill health for twenty years. She has been treated in NHS Units and a private clinic. Whilst in the private clinic it was suggested that we, as a family, might benefit from therapy. After much discussion and thought we agreed that it would possible be helpful. On our first meeting, the psychologist was not happy with something I said (hand on heart, I don't remember!) and asked me to leave. So the rest of the family stayed in the meeting whilst I waited in the car. My feelings were that his reaction to whatever I said was very unprofessional and his training should have allowed him to deal with things differently. We never returned!

It was therefore with some scepticism that we agreed to family therapy a second time. The sessions thus far have taken place over a four year period. Initially there was doubt and reticence.

Over a period of time these feelings have changed to those of trust and respect for our psychologist. She has enabled us to talk more openly about past events, in what feels like a safe place. I think the fact that this has/is taking place over an extended period of time has allowed us to revisit issues as many times as we felt necessary. Short term therapy would not.

This has been a huge commitment on/for all of us, and there have been times when I have wavered and thought this is too painful. However, changes are being made and that can only be of benefit to the whole of my family, changes, I believe, that would not have happened other than over an extended period.

The therapeutic work needed to help family members to consolidate desired relational changes can take as long as, or much longer than the processes of formulation and intervention. Trust in change can be fragile and may need committed and persistent support, when relapse or falling back into old solutions feels safer than taking renewed risks. Repetition and rehearsal through supported enactment and re-enactment provides the practice and felt security needed to go on. Here the therapist also needs persistent support from colleagues and/or supervisors to stay with the process, to manage the disappointment and to not lose heart!

Empathy

The experience of empathy is probably the most researched aspect of inter-personal trust. However, most of the research takes place in the context of individual psychotherapy. When working long term with family members' relationships there are many opportunities to deepen empathic responding through action. For example, the constant affirmation of family members' experiences in relation to each other that helps to both clarify and process experience. The repeated experience of careful listening, where people feel deeply heard promotes comforting and enables acceptance of the experiences of the other. Such listening provides a profound sense of containment and in this context it becomes possible to take emotional risks and explore the leading edge of experience. Opportunities to slow down the pace and rhythm of the sessions helps family members to both organise and re-integrate their warded off memories and experiences—their thoughts, feelings, bodily sensations, intentions and actions. Slowly, we see an emergence of a healing and more coherent narrative—one in which people have joined together to explore relational meanings, values and priorities in a way that helps them know how to go on.

In Conclusion

To conclude this chapter, I hope I have shown how, for some people, it takes longer and it is harder to build and re-build trust when the source of danger is in the room with you! The people we love can be both the source of, and the solution to, our relational difficulties. In some respects it can be easier to rebuild trust in relationships when we work, as clients, with individual therapists. If partners and family members have not experienced security and safe attachment in their earlier relationships, the therapy needs to develop their foundational resilience so that with the emergence of trust they can then contemplate and begin to take emotional risks with each other. Systemic therapy hosts "fast" models of therapeutic change within its repertoire of short-term therapeutic work. Here though, we recognise that some couples and families need a "slow burn" model of change, and in this book, we hope we can show how a systemic approach can pace and adapt to these rhythms.

Acknowledgements I have permission from Sonia, Elsa and Dinesh, and Chris and Jaqui, to use their extracts as provided for the purposes of this chapter. To them, I give my grateful thanks.

References

Gottman, J. (2011). *The science of trust.* New York: Norton.

Johnson, S. (2002). *Emotionally focused therapy with trauma survivors: Strengthening attachment bonds.* New York: Guildford.

Siegel, D., & Solomon, M. (Eds.). (2003). *Healing Trauma: Attachment, mind, body and brain.* New York: Norton.

Van der Kolk, B. (2014). *The body keeps the score* (2nd ed.). New York: Penguin.

2

Couples with Chronic Illness: Challenges and Opportunities in the Long-Term Therapeutic Relationship

Jim Sheehan

When systemic therapists embark upon a new therapeutic relationship with an individual, couple or family they do not know in that beginning the duration of the relationship they will make with those seeking their assistance. While a mixture of client expectations and assumptions embedded in the systemic psychotherapy tradition may endow the therapeutic system with an unspoken understanding of the work ahead as relatively short-term, in practice many therapeutic relationships turn out to be long-term relationships spanning across several years. This chapter explores the challenges and opportunities faced by the systemic therapist in one particular therapeutic context namely, the help-seeking couple with a chronic illness in one or both members-where the work often proves to be long-term. The first section of the chapter briefly reviews the range of chronic illnesses systemic therapists find in those couples seeking assistance. It also offers an overview of the links between chronic Illness and the couple relationship before considering the relevance of

J. Sheehan (✉)
Family Therapy and Systemic Practice,
VID Specialized University, Oslo, Norway

21

couple-oriented interventions in the context of chronic illness. It will reflect on the reasons some couples experiencing chronic illness seem able to capitalise on the opportunities attaching to the illness to strengthen and develop their couple bond without the need for therapeutic assistance while a second group of couples require therapeutic assistance in the short-term. A third group of couples, however, seek and require assistance over much longer periods of time. It is the long-term therapy of this group of chronic illness couples that is the focus of this chapter. Section "Building and Maintaining Attachment in Long-Term Systemic Therapy" of the chapter describes some of the challenges involved in building and maintaining a therapeutic bond with couples over long periods of time. It will focus upon a set of features and principles that often characterise the building and maintaining of the therapeutic bond with couples that must be durable in the long term. The third and final part of the chapter reviews the range of roles and systemic perspectives which may be adopted by practitioners in this area of long-term therapy. The limitations of these perspectives for addressing certain aspects of the work is underlined as is the importance of drawing upon practice perspectives lying beyond those traditionally understood to belong to the family of systemic models. In this review of usable perspectives emphasis is placed upon both the solvable and non-solvable concerns faced within the long-term therapeutic work. The conclusion to the chapter offers some brief reflections on the demands and opportunities built in to the long-term supervisory relationships that often accompany this area of long-term therapeutic practice.

Couples, Chronic Illness and Long-Term Systemic Therapy

The chronic conditions that accompany couples into therapy include multiple sclerosis, arthritis, emphysema, cardiovascular disease, cancer, chronic pain, stroke, renal failure and cerebral palsy. This list is far from exhaustive and some couples carry more than one chronic condition between them. Chronic illness arrives in the life of a couple as a third

element whose enduring presence may command almost constant attention. Such illnesses are like uninvited guests that threaten to take over a
couple's home and to rearrange the furniture of couple life. As a third
element in the relationship, an element that often grows in strength over
time, chronic illness may transform the identity of the couple through
the gradual confiscation of some of their most cherished rituals. Depending upon the behaviour of the illness it may tease the couple into believing it has gone on a long vacation only to arrive 'home' unexpectedly
to retake central position on the couple and family stage. Depending
upon couple history its arrival may herald the commencement of an
apprenticeship in the endurance of previously unknown levels of physical, psychological/emotional and relational suffering. As a suffering unto
death chronic illness gradually changes the voice of mortality in the ear
of the couple from a soft-spoken whisper to a resounding gong, reminding couple members of the passing of their suffering bodies, lives and
relationships.

If the above description bears witness to some of the most difficult
consequences of chronic illness for some couples it by no means tells the
full story of the impact of chronic illness on couple life. Rolland (1994),
for example, underlines the crisis character inherent in the arrival of
chronic illness. Some couples manage to transform the challenges posed
by an illness into opportunities for growth and development in their relationship. But the possibility of such positive coping responses is seen by
some (Lyons et al. 1995) as dependant on the couple's ability to see different illness-related challenges as 'our' challenge rather than 'yours' or
'mine' or by others (Berg-Cross 1997) as related to a couple's capacity to
seize the opportunity of the illness to communicate at a deeper level and
thus strengthen the couple bond. Kowal et al. (2003) summarised the
state of our knowledge at the turn of the twenty-first century about the
impact of chronic illness on the couple by proposing that while the onset
and course of chronic illness can have problematic effects on patients,
their partners and their relationships such events and their sequelae do
not necessarily have a detrimental influence on couples. Long-term therapy with couples with chronic illness, however, bears witness to the fact
that a group of couples, for a variety of reasons this chapter section will

later consider, are seriously impacted over the long term by the conditions that strike them.

What are the known connections in the two-way relationship between chronic illness and couple relationship? When the impact of the couple relationship on chronic illness is considered it has been suggested that the married status of a couple impacts positively both mortality rates (Berkman and Syme 1976) and survival rates once a chronic illness has been diagnosed (Gordon and Rosenthal 1995). It has also been shown that higher compliance levels with medical regimes are more likely to be present in married rather than unmarried couples (Goodwin et al. 1987) and that separated and divorced partners display lower levels of immune function than those who are married (Kiecolt-Glaser et al. 1987). However, it has also been proposed that, regardless of being married, the presence of conflict within the chronic illness couple may have a negative impact on health outcomes through the restriction of partners' ability to seek support (Coyne and DeLongis 1986). Marital distress has also been shown to be associated with impaired immune system function which is, in turn, linked to physical illness, disease and poor health outcomes (Kiecolt-Glaser et al. 1987, 1988, 1993, 1997). More specifically, negative interaction between couple members has been associated with a variety of health problems (Gottman 1994) and critical remarks by intimate partners are also known to adversely affect disease activity and a patient's capacity to cope with chronic illness (Manne 1999). The presence of a supportive partner is also associated with lower levels of pain medication use and reduced incidences of rehospitalisation of the patient (Kulik and Mahler 1989).

When we consider the impact of chronic illness on the couple relationship we have already noted that this does not necessarily materialise in negative outcomes. A type of couple response referred to by some researchers (Lyons et al. 1998) as 'communal coping' may well be the key to understanding why the crisis of chronic illness may be transformed by some couples into an opportunity for growth in the relationship rather than a precursor to relationship deterioration. Some studies (e.g. Schmaling and Sher 1997) have shown that chronic physical illness may either decrease, increase or be neutral with respect to marital satisfaction levels. Other studies (e.g. Burman and Margolin 1992) have suggested that such differences in outcomes may be related to the type of illness involved as well as to the characteristics within each illness such as the degree of severity and chronicity. An important finding is that of Helgeson (1993) who showed that chronic illnesses can greatly increase the burdens placed on patient's partners. Others have suggested that such burdens can negatively impact the level of social support experienced by patients and also bring about a reduction in the quality of the couple relationship (Coyne et al. 1987).

When it comes to the relevance of couple therapy for patients with chronic illness there is strong evidence that couple-oriented interventions impact the wellbeing of patients in a number of ways. In a cross-disease review of the findings from thirty-three studies evaluating couple-oriented interventions for chronic physical illness, Martire et al. (2010) found that couple-oriented interventions had significant effects on patient depressive symptoms, marital functioning and pain and were more efficacious than either patient psychosocial interventions or usual care. These researchers concluded that the small effects of couple-oriented interventions can be strengthened by targeting partners' influence on patient health behaviours and focusing on couples with high illness-related conflict, low partner support and low overall marital quality. Indeed, in this writer's experience it is the focus on these elements that form the substance of much therapeutic work, of whatever length, with couples carrying the burden of a chronic illness. Systemic therapists engaged with the chronic illness couple will attempt to reduce or resolve illness-related couple conflict, increase levels of partner support and improve the quality of couple interaction.

If, as has been shown above, the part played by the couple relationship in impacting a variety of chronic illness outcome variables has been well established as has the relative efficacy of couple-oriented interventions in assisting couples with a broad range of chronic illnesses, why, then, do some couples struggling with chronic illness seem to require relatively long-term therapeutic assistance while others appear to cope well with either moderate amounts of the same assistance or no therapeutic assistance at all? The general lacuna in research into long-term systemic therapy strikes this area of clinical practice just as it does other practice domains. Hence, the responses offered here to this question are based upon the clinical experiences of the writer with this population as well as upon the experiences of practitioners encountered in supervision. The hypothesis proposed rests upon the reality that chronic illness arrives in the lives of unique couples with unique couple and individual histories. While the practical challenges of the same chronic illness may be much the same for a broad range of receiving couples the relative depth of the psychological/emotional and relational challenges experienced can be impacted by couple history factors such as periods of domestic violence, infidelity, addiction, periods of couple separation, or intermittent mental health crises and by individual history factors such as abuse-related childhood traumas, the loss of primary attachment figures in childhood, experiences of sexual violence in young adulthood and insecure attachment styles developed in childhood and persisting unmodified into adult relational life. Couples requiring long-term therapeutic assistance may well carry a number of these couple and individual historical factors between them. And they may well have had relatively short-term and unsatisfactory experiences of couple therapy in their past. Challenges associated with their attachment styles may well have led to premature exits from prior therapies without such exits ever leading to the final cessation of the couple relationship. Ironically, the persistence of psychological/relational challenges associated with the practical challenges of the illness may be one factor which keeps the couple in therapy long enough to forge an incrementally greater level of trust with a persevering therapist. Where such therapeutic bonds are forged and developed over time it is difficult to escape the observation that it may be the very longevity of illness-related therapy that provides the opportunity for a greater level of individual healing from childhood traumas as well as a greater level of relational healing of past, but still living, wounds from a couple's own unique history. How, then, does the systemic therapist create the best opportunity for forging a therapeutic bond with couples needing assistance over the long term that maximises the possibilities both for creative responses to illness challenges and for the healing of wounds of different kinds in couple and individual histories.

Building and Maintaining Attachment in Long-Term Systemic Therapy

While the systemic therapist must build an attachment with clients in the context of therapeutic work of varying lengths, most of this work is relatively short-term and may last for anything from a single consultation to a ten- or twenty-session piece of work across a 12-month period. And, while there is nothing inherent in chronic illness itself which automatically propels the struggling couple into long-term therapeutic work, in practice the trajectory and variations built in to the illnesses noted above bring challenges to many couples who feel unable, for the additional reasons mentioned in the previous section, to address such challenges without therapeutic assistance over the longer-term. At the commencement of such couple therapy relationships their long-term character cannot be known. It is only over time that the work and the therapeutic relationship are revealed as long-term. But what are the characteristics of these long-term attachment bonds that are built across time and what might they require of the therapist? How are they the same or different from the attachments that form the basis of short-term therapeutic relationships? Four such characteristics are noted here.

Availability

When couple therapy in the context of chronic illness moves across that borderline, however specified, that separates relatively short-term work from that which is becoming relatively long-term, something happens to the availability of the therapist within the therapy system. In short-term systemic psychotherapy, where the goals are often clear and singular, the therapist commits to a level of availability that is worked out between therapist and clients at the commencement of therapy and is judged by both to be adequate for the therapeutic task at hand. And, very often, this task finds completion in one way or another, and with one outcome or another, without any alteration to the frequency level of sessions or to the implicit or explicit rules about between-sessions calls with the therapist. By contrast, the couple and their therapist who have travelled some distance into the territory of longer-term work have been through some crises associated with the multiple and changing demands of a specific illness and have learned together something about the differential challenges such variations constitute for each of the couple members and why. These shared passages through the different times of an illness create an awareness within the therapeutic system of the need for an extended availability on the part of the therapist, whether in the form of slightly longer, or more frequent, sessions in addition to availability on the telephone in specific circumstances. Such extended availability is not necessarily a permanent modification to the therapeutic contract and should always keep in mind what the therapist can practically and emotionally deliver as well as what the clients may need. In extending their availability the therapist also needs to keep in mind the therapeutic importance of maintaining the boundary point of such extended availability no matter how needy and/or despairing either of the couple members may appear to be at a moment in time.

While extended therapist availability, in the guise of variations in session frequency and between session calls, maybe a necessary characteristic of many different contexts of long-term therapy, it is reflective of, but not a substitution for, another type of therapist availability that is central to long-term work with couples in the context of chronic illness. This is empathic availability described first by the existentialist philosopher, Marcel (1956, 1963), and later perceived by Lantz (1996) as a critical component in the psychotherapy of chronic illness couples. Through their empathic availability the therapist brings to the exchange an openness to the couple's pain and suffering and this type of availability shows itself in the therapist's capacity to be 'touched' or 'moved' by the different kinds of suffering couple members must endure.

Flexibility

A second characteristic required of the therapist in longer-term work with the couple in the context of chronic illness is flexibility in the delivery of the therapy. Such flexibility can take many different forms. It may mean meeting with the 'healthy' partner alone when the 'ill' member is unable to be at a session, or vice versa. Or it can mean having the couple session with one member of the couple physically present with the therapist while the other member participates 'on speaker' or on 'Skype' from a hospital bed. Or it can mean changing the location of the therapy to a hospital room when a hospitalisation period becomes longer than anticipated. Flexibility may also apply to the level of therapy fees charged where the therapy services are neither state-funded nor covered by health insurance. In such instances the different financial costs of managing a chronic illness need to be borne in mind by the therapist who may offer reduced fees for periods of time when couple sessions need to be more frequent for whatever reason.

Variations in Intensity

Doing long-term systemic therapy with chronic illness couples sometimes feels like being in the middle of a marathon walk or run of indeterminate length. For large periods of time the pace may be steady, the frequency of meetings predictable and the challenges manageable. But, periodically, crises occur which require a change of therapeutic tempo, an injection of pace and an increase in intensity. The 'healthy' partner may feel overwhelmed and no longer able to cope with the unrelenting demands of an illness and announce that they want to leave the relationship. Or an unexpected and sudden loss of functionality in the 'ill' member of the couple may present both with a set of challenges for which they feel completely unprepared. These contexts often bring their own panic to couple members and require alterations in therapeutic intensity and/or changes in the frequency of therapy sessions. Therapeutic meetings happening at a frequency of either once or twice per month must quickly transform to a frequency of once or twice per week depending upon the nature of the crisis. It is in these unpredictable times of crisis for the couple and demands for response from the therapist that the underlying contract between couple and therapist is transformed. The therapist effectively deepens their commitment to the couple and says by their responsiveness: 'I will be with you in every way I can, and as you need, to help you meet whatever challenges lie ahead'.

Therapist commitment to availability and flexibility, demonstrated through crisis periods, can be the gateway to a deeper attachment and a deeper level of trust in the therapeutic relationship with the chronic illness couple. Such commitment can also be the vehicle through which the healing embedded in the therapeutic attachment can impact earlier trauma in the lives of one or both couple members. Chronic illness arrives equally in the lives of those with secure or insecure attachment histories. For those couple members with insecure attachment histories, resulting from whatever range of problematic childhood circumstances, the long-term therapeutic relationship associated with the challenges of chronic illness may offer opportunities for the progressive healing of trauma that might not otherwise occur.

Six years in to the management of her husband Bill's chronic kidney disease Clodagh told him that she had 'had enough' and was leaving the relationship. Within 24 hours she had packed some bags and departed for her sister's holiday home some 150 kilometres away. Clodagh and Bill had been meeting twice per month with their therapist over the previous three years and dealing with a broad range of challenges his illness presented to them individually and as a couple. One theme they had been addressing was Clodagh's exhaustion from the range of physical demands that Bill's illness placed upon her as the only other member of the household. Clodagh had literally turned her life inside out in terms of work, friendships and leisure activities in order to make possible the management of Bill's illness at home. Despite encouragement from the therapist and Bill to plan a break period for herself Clodagh felt unable to respond to this suggestion, saying that she 'knew' that Bill's family and their friends expected it of her as his wife that she be there 24/7 to meet whatever of Bill's needs he was unable to meet on his own. Within three days of her departure a crisis therapy session occurred, attended by both Clodagh and Bill, in which the therapist and Bill both validated Clodagh's feelings and reasons for leaving the relationship. Bill made it clear that he loved Clodagh and that, while he did not want to separate, he knew that the demands placed on he at home by virtue of his illness were intolerable and were destroying her and her life. The therapist encouraged Bill to put an 'alert' out to their own adult children, his own siblings and the local healthcare team that were assisting with the management of Bill's condition. Over the next month the therapist held weekly sessions with the couple and an additional weekly session with Clodagh who expressed surprise that the therapist continued to validate her right to a life for herself and not just a life whose contours would be specified by the evolving demands of Bill's deteriorating condition. Within a month two of their adult children and one of his siblings had come 'on board' to help Bill for specific parts of the week. In addition, the local healthcare team regraded his priority status for the receipt of additional resources. In the weeks following her decision to return home to her husband Clodagh developed a deeper bond with the therapist and began to use some of the couple therapy time to work through her feelings of abandonment and rejection that had arisen following the departure of her mother from home when she was 12 years old, leaving herself and her father to look after four younger siblings.

Loyalty/Solidarity

Therapy over the longer-term means that just as the therapist meets the clients through many phases of their coping and not coping with different illness-related challenges the clients also meet the therapist across many aspects of his or her life. They may meet the therapist in the sun-filled light of summer mornings or in the darkness of cold winter evenings, before holidays when they seem tired and in need of a break or after holidays when they seem alive and re-energised, or when the therapist must take a break for a period because of a pregnancy, birth, illness or bereavement in their own life. In short, when the long-term therapeutic relationship remains an alive and engaged encounter (Katz and Shotter 2003) clients and therapist get to know each other in a much deeper way and something grows between them that exceeds the description of the relationship as the performance of a therapeutic contract. Words this writer uses for this excess are loyalty and solidarity. Solidarity reflects a deeply human, shoulder-to-shoulder, the relationship between people who know that, despite the specific set of circumstances that defines their relationship at a moment in time, they are both subject to the pain, suffering, joy and loss that strikes each unique human life. An experience of solidarity, arising from an awareness of a shared humanity, can be one of the benefits of the long-term therapeutic relationship for clients and therapists alike. This writer encountered an experience of solidarity recently while saying goodbye at the end of a session to a couple, in therapy for three years, where one member is suffering from cancer at an advanced stage. The out of season hydrangea that graced the garden adjacent to the therapy room was tied up but remained with their dying heads on. While the couple exulted with the therapist at the beauty of the in-season white hydrangea they quietly advised that the flowers would probably do better next season if the dead heads were now cut off. The advice was graciously received and the dead heads were cut off the same evening. There is, indeed, a season for everything.

Systemic Frameworks in Long-Term Therapeutic Work with Chronic Illness Couples

The onset of chronic illness may unbalance a couple's relationship with each other as well as catapulting them into new networks of relationship outside their immediate couple world and in which they experience having little or no control. Their journey with the illness may require their therapist to take up many different roles informed by different systemic frameworks and perspectives. The practitioner must act at times as a *couple therapist* with interventions aimed solely at the couple relationship itself. At other moments during the work they may act as a *systemic consultant* helping the couple consider how they position themselves in relation to medical, health and social service providers in order to access the resources that they need at that time. During other phases of the work the systemic practitioner will be a *family therapist* focusing on the way the three generations of family relationships have adjusted to the illness and its varying demands. And, finally, the practitioner may adopt a *narrative therapy* perspective as their attention is directed towards individual identity concerns as the course of an illness and its demands causes havoc with couple members' sense of who they are.

The onset and development of chronic Illness can create levels of dependency on a partner and on others that were previously unknown in the couple relationship and fall far outside the comfort zone of either the ill person or their partner. The patient may have been abused or neglected in childhood and developed a survival script lasting into adult life in which coping alone forms a major plank. In such contexts the systemic therapist, as couple therapist, immediately finds themselves on ground where the requirement for the couple to expand the ways they coordinate cycles of dependence and independence in the relationship dovetails with the need for the patient to revise their survival script sufficiently to enable the growth of greater trust in the partner which in turn may allow the illness to be managed better in the home setting. Systemic perspectives such as Emotionally Focused Couple Therapy (Johnston 2002) and Attachment Narrative Therapy (Dallos 2006; Dallos and Vetere 2009) can be invaluable resources for practitioners addressing such challenges. Similarly, the patient's need for medical and health interventions and care make them dependent on a group of professionals whose less than perfect performance and coordination can reactivate panic and anxiety in the person dependent upon them for assistance. In such instances the therapist practitioner must find a way to contain levels of emotional arousal in the patient at the same time as drawing upon systemic consultancy perspectives which might facilitate the re-positioning of the couple in their relationship with service providers.

The management of many chronic illnesses often require the resources of more than one generation. The degree of functionality of the couple's relationship with their adult children and grandchildren may contribute positively, or not at all, to the quality of life of the ill person and their partner. A long-term therapy which attempts to engage three generations may open possibilities for the further healing of wounds in the relationship between adult children and their parents. Indeed, a small degree of additional healing arising from consultations between parents and adult children, who may have suffered in their childhood from problematic parenting behaviours, can generate new patterns of mutual assistance between parents and children at the same time as transforming dormant grandparent/grandchild relationships into living and engaged relationships.

Finally, chronic illness can place such demands on the couple and its members by turning their lives upside-down and inside-out in a host of different ways. The management of the illness may require periodic alterations in work schedules from full-time to part-time to no work at all and back through this cycle again. It also may involve interruptions to recreational patterns, decreased capacity to fulfil friendship, parental or grandparental obligations as well as periodic or permanent incapacity to enjoy a range of couple rituals such as vacations abroad, a meal in a restaurant or a trip to the local cinema. In the context of such changes and losses individuals often grapple painfully with disruptions in the self's relationship to self. They wonder, despairingly, about who and what they have become individually and as a couple. In addressing such questions the systemic therapist may draw upon perspectives such as narrative therapy (White and Epston 1990; Sheehan 1999; White 2007) that explicitly deal with themes of personal identity and individual's experiences of continuity and change in their sense of self across time.

Solvable and Non-solvable Concerns

While the systemic practitioner can draw upon an array of elegant systemic frameworks in the search for solutions to many of the dilemmas faced by the couple burdened by chronic illness there are some couple anxieties and concerns that call for acceptance and forbearance rather than a search for solutions. The emotional, psychological and relational suffering associated with physical pain and the loss of functionality, the sense of death drawing near and the struggle to find meaning in the face of such realities are three such contexts where the practitioner may draw upon spiritual or therapeutic perspectives not normally considered part of the family of systemic models as they accompany the couple facing such anxieties and challenges. While the different cultures to which client couples and systemic practitioners belong endow these experiences with their own unique meaning, attention is drawn here to one such therapeutic model that may enrich the systemic practitioner's way of being with couples facing such experiences and realities. This perspective is Existential Psychotherapy (Lantz 1978; Lantz and Alford 1995; Lantz 1996).

Developed in the final decades of the twentieth-century Existential Psychotherapy finds its theoretical base in the existential concepts of Victor Frankl (1959, 1969), an Austrian psychiatrist, and Gabriel Marcel (1951, 1956, 1963), a French philosopher. As a therapeutic approach with couples facing chronic illness the perspective places emphasis on the human encounter between therapists and clients, the growth opportunities for client couples in the engagement with crises, the dimensions of freedom and responsibility throughout the therapy and the basic human desire to find and experience a degree of meaning and purpose in intimate life (Lantz 1996). The approach invites practitioners to guard against an overly strategic and problem-solving disposition in therapeutic work and to place emphasis on what Marcel refers to as 'testimony'. Testimony, in contrast to an objectivist type of observation of couple patterns and behaviours, refers to the therapist's capacity to report on the impact of the encounter with client others on themselves and fosters the emergence in the therapist of a relational type of existence based upon love, participation and fidelity (Lantz 1999; Marcel 1973). Finally, the existential approach focuses on certain aspects of human experience as mysteries to be encountered rather than problems to be solved. In responding to clients' search for meaning in the face of illness, intense suffer and the inevitability of death the approach appreciate these experiences as perplexities that shake us, therapists and clients alike, make us sleepless and evade our mastery.

Supervisory Adjustments in the Context of Long-Term Therapeutic Contracts

How can the supervisory relationship best assist the systemic practitioner in their long-term therapy with couples facing chronic illness? While there are many factors which shape the supervisory relationship in this context—most notably, the experience level of the practitioner with respect to couple therapy but also the degree of knowledge they possess about the chronic illness being managed—the relationship needs, where possible, to mirror many of the characteristics of the therapy itself. It is helpful, but not always essential or feasible, if the supervisory relationship can remain without interruption across the whole period of long-term couple therapy. Just as the longevity of the therapeutic bond with the couple allows that bond to grow in strength with accompanying opportunities noted in an earlier section of this chapter, so the bond formed within the supervisory relationship has an opportunity to deepen over time and such depth brings with it opportunities for the personal and professional development of both practitioner and supervisor (Sheehan 2016).

There are two particular ways in which long-term supervision can assist practitioners working with couples in the context of chronic illness. The first concerns the fact that the work is often simply very difficult and can have a one-step-forward-two-steps-backwards feel at times. This facet of the work can be very draining even for the experienced practitioner and it is not unusual for practitioners to feel a sense of hopelessness and despair in the face of so much therapeutic effort and so little evident progress towards an agreed goal. Just as the feelings of the couple in long-term therapy can oscillate between hope and despair, thus obliging their therapist to 'hold hope' (Flaskas 2007) for them when they are in the despair part of this arc, so the supervisor needs to 'hold hope' for the practitioner when they experience feelings of hopelessness about the efficacy of the work, feelings which often drive them to want a speedy conclusion to the work. These are the moments when the supervisor must remind the practitioner, in the warmest and most supportive way possible, that the work is having its therapeutic effect even if there has not yet been a resolution to the most recently experienced couple conflict. The supervisor must remind themselves and the practitioner that incremental healing flows from the therapeutic relationship itself and not simply from the therapy's capacity to find solutions to current dilemmas. Sometimes just keeping going is a critical part of the work!

A second way in which the supervisor can assist the longer-term work can arrive when the couple reach moments in the course of an illness when the illness, through ever-reducing functionality in the ill person, appears to have stripped the relationship of most of its daily and weekly rituals. In the grip of intense physical and emotional suffering, heightened awareness of the possibility of death drawing near and deeper kinds of questioning about the meaning of their current lives and relation-ship, the couple need a practitioner who can find a way to be with them and support them in the middle of their suffering, losses and anguished search for meaning. The long-term supervisor is well positioned to assist the practitioner and the therapy at this point by creating a supported space in which the practitioner can reflect upon their own relationship and engagement with physical suffering, loss, mortality and meaning in their own unique life. The encounter with these themes may encourage both the systemic practitioner and supervisor to reach towards practice models like existential psychotherapy (Lantz 1994, 1996), described in the previous section, that deal more explicitly with such themes and chal-lenges as a complement to the variety of systemic frameworks already informing their work.

Conclusion

This chapter has considered some of the challenges and opportunities facing systemic practitioners as they engage with a group of couples, bur-dened with chronic illness, who for different reasons require long-term systemic therapy. Some aspects of what it takes to build and maintain attachment in the therapeutic relationship over the long-term have been described as has the opportunity for further healing of past individual or relational wounds arising from the longevity character of the chronic illness-related couple therapy. The variety of roles adopted by systemic practitioners in the course of longer-term work was also considered and the chapter described how the sequentially adopted roles of couple ther-apist, systemic consultant, family therapist and narrative therapist cre-ated opportunities for transformations in the couple relationship itself, the couple's relationship with service providers, three-generational family relationships and the personal identities of couple members. The chapter also proposed that in this type of long-term systemic therapy practition-ers may find it enriching to draw upon therapeutic frameworks not tradi-tionally viewed as part of the family of systemic models as a complement to the range of systemic frameworks already described. In this regard, attention was drawn to the potential relevance of Existential Psychotherapy for the domain of long-term systemic practice under consideration. Finally, the chapter explored a parallel set of opportunities and challenges arising in long-term supervisory relationships supporting practitioners in this area of practice.

References

Berg-Cross, I. (1997). *Couples therapy*. Thousand Oaks, CA: Sage.

Berkman, L. F., & Syme, S. L. (1976). Social networks, host resistance and mortality: A nine-year follow-up study of Alameda County residents. *Journal of Epidemiology, 109*, 186–204.

Burman, B., & Margolin, G. (1992). Analysis of the association between marital relationships and health problems: An interactional perspective. *Psychology Bulletin, 112*, 39–63.

Coyne, J. C., & DeLongis, A. (1986). Going beyond social support: The role of social relationships in adaptation. *Journal of Consulting and Clinical Psychology, 54*, 454–460.

Coyne, J., Kessler, R., Tal, M., Turnbull, J., Wortman, C., & Greden, J. (1987). Living with a depressed person. *Journal of Consulting and Clinical Psychology, 55*, 347–352.

Dallos, R. (2006). *Attachment narrative therapy: Integrating narrative, systemic and attachment therapies*. Maidenhead: Open University Press/McGraw-Hill.

Dallos, R., & Vetere, A. (2009). *Systemic therapy and attachment narratives: Applications in a range of clinical settings*. London: Routledge.

Flaskas, C. (2007). The balance of hope and hopelessness. In C. Flaskas, I. McCarthy, & J. Sheehan (Eds.), *Hope and despair in narrative and family therapy* (pp. 24–35). London: Routledge.

Frankl, V. (1959). *From death camp to existentialism*. Boston: Beacon Hill Press.

Frankl, V. (1969). *The will to meaning*. New York: New American Library.

Goodwin, J. S., Hunt, W. C., Key, C. R., & Samet, J. M. (1987). The effect of marital status on stage, treatment, and survival of cancer patients. *Journal of the American Medical Association, 258*, 3125–3130.

Gordon, H. S., & Rosenthal, G. E. (1995). Impact of marital status on outcome in hospitalized patients. *Archives of Internal Medicine, 155*, 2465–2471.

Gottman, J. (1994). *What predicts divorce?* Hillsdale, NJ: Erlbaum.

Helgeson, V. S. (1993). The onset of chronic illness: Its effect on the patient-spouse relationship. *Journal of Social and Clinical Psychology, 12*, 406–428.

Johnson, S. (2002). *Emotionally-focused couple therapy with trauma survivors: Strengthening emotional bonds.* New York: Guilford.

Katz, A. M., & Shotter, J. (2003). Methods of a 'social poetics' in people becoming present to each other and to themselves. In G. Larner & D. Pare (Eds.), *Critical knowledge in psychology and psychotherapy.* New York: Haworth Press.

Kiecolt-Glaser, J. K., Fisher, I. D., Ogrocki, P., Stout, J. C., Speicher, C. F., & Glaser, R. (1987). Marital quality, marital disruption and immune functioning. *Psychosomatic Medicine, 49,* 13–34.

Kiecolt-Glaser, J. K., Glaser, R., Cacciopo, J. T., MacCullum, R. C., & Snydersmith, M. (1997). Marital conflict in older adults: Endocrine and immunological correlates. *Psychosomatic Medicine, 59,* 339–349.

Kiecolt-Glaser, J. K., Kennedy, S., Malkoff, S., Fisher, L., Speicher, C. F., & Glaser, R. (1988). Marital discord and immunity in males. *Psychosomatic Medicine, 50,* 213–219.

Kiecolt-Glaser, J. K., Malarkey, W. B., Chee, M., Newton, T., & Cacioppo, J. T. (1993). Negative behaviour during marital conflict is associated with immunological down-regulation. *Psychosomatic Medicine, 55,* 395–409.

Kowal, J., Johnson, S. M., & Lee, A. (2003). Chronic illness in couples: A case for emotionally focused therapy. *Journal of Marital and Family Therapy, 29*(3), 299–310.

Kulik, J. A., & Mahler, H. I. M. (1989). Social support and recovery from surgery. *Health Psychology, 8,* 221–238.

Lantz, J. (1978). *Family and marital therapy.* New York: Appleton-Century-Crofts.

Lantz, J. (1994). Marcel's 'availability' in existential psychotherapy with couples and families. *Contemporary Family Therapy, 16*(6), 489–501.

Lantz, J. (1996). Existential psychotherapy with chronic illness couples. *Contemporary Family Therapy, 18*(2), 197–208.

Lantz, J. (1999). Marcel's testimony in existential psychotherapy with couples and families. *Contemporary Family Therapy, 21*(4), 469–483.

Lantz, J., & Alford, K. (1995). Existential family therapy with an urban-Appalachian adolescent. *Journal of Family Psychotherapy, 6,* 15–27.

Lyons, R. F., Mickelson, K. D., Sullivan, M. J. I., & Coyne, J. C. (1998). Coping as a communal process. *Journal of Social and Personal Relationships, 15,* 579–605.

Lyons, R. F., Sullivan, M. J. I., & Ritvo, P. G. (1995). *Relationships in chronic illness and disability.* Thousand Oaks, CA: Sage.

Manne, S. L. (1999). Intrusive thoughts and psychological distress among cancer patients: The role of spouse avoidance and criticism. *Journal of Consulting and Clinical Psychology, 67*(4), 539–546.

Marcel, G. (1951). *Homo viator.* Chicago: Henry Regenery.

Marcel, G. (1956). *The philosophy of existence.* New York: Citadel Press.

Marcel, G. (1963). *The existential background of human dignity.* Cambridge, MA: Harvard University Press.

Marcel, G. (1973). *Tragic wisdom and beyond.* Evanston: Northwestern University Press.

Martire, L. M., Schultz, R., Helgeson, V. S., Small, B. J., & Saghafi, E. M. (2010). Review and meta-analysis of couple-oriented interventions for chronic illness. *Annals of Behavioural Medicine, 40*(3), 325–342.

Rolland, J. S. (1994). In sickness and in health: The impact of illness on couples' relationships. *Journal of Marital and Family Therapy, 20,* 327–347.

Schmaling, K. B., & Sher, T. G. (1997). Physical health and relationships. In W. K. Halford & H. J. Markman (Eds.), *Clinical handbook of marriage and couple interventions* (pp. 323–345). Chichester, UK: Wiley.

Sheehan, J. (1999). Liberating narrational styles in systemic practice. *Journal of Systemic Therapies, 18*(3), 51–68.

Sheehan, J. (2016). Self and world: Narrating experience in the supervisor/supervisee relationship. In A. Vetere & P. Stratton (Eds.), *Interacting selves: Systemic solutions for personal and professional development in counselling and psychotherapy* (pp. 109–129). London: Routledge.

White, M. (2007). *Maps of narrative practice.* New York: Norton.

White, M., & Epston, D. (1990). *Narrative means to therapeutic ends.* New York: Norton.

Part II

Long Term Systemic Work with Individuals

3

Olena's Battle for Utopia

Chip Chimera

This is the story of a long term relationship, one of the longest I have known both personally and professionally. It is full of twists and turns and roundabouts. Some readers will read with raised eyebrows and unspoken 'tuts'. Others may see how the development of the relationship over time has been healing for both of us in a number of directions. She has given me so much as a therapist and fellow traveller. I hope that will become clear.

I want to talk about mutual influence, the wounded healer and tremendous respect for this journey: what it has taught me, how it has influenced my practice and how it has changed me as a person.

C. Chimera (✉)
Leatherhead, UK
e-mail: chipchimera@btinternet.com

© The Author(s) 2020
A. Vetere and J. Sheehan (eds.), *Long Term Systemic Therapy*,
Palgrave Texts in Counselling and Psychotherapy,
https://doi.org/10.1007/978-3-030-44511-9_3

The Beginning of the Beginning

I first met F twenty years ago when I was part of a team on a psychodrama trauma retreat. The weekend was designed for trauma survivors and the teamwork was meant to ensure safety and support.[1] I had undertaken extra training in the Therapeutic Spiral Model (Hudgins 2002) and was honoured to be part of the team of experienced therapists.

F was a participant brought by one of the other team members who had been working with her individually for a number of years. In the group she was mute, regressed and shrunk into herself. She needed one to one containment from a team member for most of the workshop. Often this was me and we made a link and a rapport. There was no pressure to speak or directly work. Just being present was work enough. My role was to help her stay grounded and psychologically present during the group's work. Outside of the therapy space F was sociable enough to make good links with one or two other participants. Once back in the group she regressed again. Although mute she could communicate in writing. We learned of the intense fear which was triggered by therapy itself, whether individually or in a group setting. She evoked in all of us, team and participants, a deep wish to help and a feeling of respectful pathos.

Following the session, she continued in therapy with my colleague.

In stark contrast to the vulnerable self we saw in the group, in the 'outside world' F was a competent and accomplished maths teacher in a challenging secondary school. There is literally safety in numbers. Numbers never let you down, they are reliable and consistent. She is skilled and whilst she could have taught the highest achievers she chooses to spend her time with those students who are struggling. She gets them through GCSEs and celebrates their achievements. It is hard to connect the self-confident and fearless maths teacher with the shy and struggling client self we met in the therapy space.

Two or three years passed. F's father died. She returned to live near her mother, coincidentally in my neck of the woods, getting a job in a

---

[1] Having completed systemic psychotherapy training I then looked around for another training which included an understanding of individual development and was also 'systemic friendly'. Psychodrama fit this bill and I qualified in 2003.

local comprehensive. She made contact and we reconnected. F sought therapy with me having made a good connection in the previous group. She began attending my psychodrama group. She came to three sessions, then abruptly stopped. It was too difficult. I offered individual work but that was not possible for her at the time.

More time passed, another year at least. F rang out of the blue and asked to start therapy again. We arranged to meet. At the appointed time she texted me saying she was in the car park but couldn't come in. She was frozen at the thought of therapy. She had wanted to come but just couldn't. I rushed out to the car park to try to help her in but she was gone by the time I got there.

More time passed. About two years later I received another text: 'I am really ready now.' And she was.

The death of F's father had been a watershed. She had stayed near her mother, met another teacher at the school and married. She was in a different place and definitely ready to begin the journey she had been longing to make and had known she needed in order to make sense of her experiences (for F the death of her father was crucial—so long as he was alive he was living proof of the futility of trying to recover).

Theory box 3.1 Throughout this work, I have drawn on my broader systemic training and particularly the Coordinated Management of Meaning (Pearce and Littlejohn 1997; Pearce 2007, 2012). I have also drawn heavily on theories of developmental trauma (van der Kolk 2013), the Therapeutic Spiral Model of trauma treatment (Hudgins 2002) and Crittenden's model of attachment: the Dynamic Maturational Model (2008/2016).

These boxes are intended to highlight particular aspects of theory that seemed relevant at the stage of work.

Initially, I was aware of the work of John Byng-Hall (1995) in relation to the creation of a safe space in therapy, going at the client's pace and having great respect for the client's defences. Crittenden (personal communication) has said that going into therapy is one of the most dangerous things a trauma survivor can do: putting yourself into the hands

> of a human being, when other humans have betrayed your trust so fundamentally is an act of courage.

Olena's Battle for Utopia. (Written by F aged 14/15, Olena being an anagram of 'Alone'.)

The laughter was enhancing the beauty of the warm, bright summer evening as the men played their game of back garden cricket. Olena was sitting on her bedroom windowsill, analysing every action, every run, every shout of excitement. By her side can be found her two closest companions, Blackie and Queenie. Everyone who understood a small child's love for her friends would realise that Queenie was most definitely the favourite. Once a fluffy, white and glistening coat, but now grey and flattened with undying love. Queenie was always there for Olena: always listened, never left, never judged.

'You're out' exclaimed Jim, as he hastily grabbed the Slazenger Sixe 5. 'It's my turn'. Paul looked a little uneasy, never finding sporting failures comfortable. They looked so much like the best of friends, despite the clear competitive streak in all three of them. Olena was learning the rules, the strokes, hoping that one day she'd be able to be a part of the one day Test matches that graced the garden. 'When you're older', 'you'll be allowed one day'.

Every child dreams yet all children's frustration. People should learn not to wish their days away, but they do, they live for their tomorrows. But, if we knew what our tomorrows held, would we really choose to live for them?

Beginning Proper

Like all good systemic work we started with a genogram (McGoldrick et al. 2008) (Fig. 3.1).

Here is where we started, the basic social ggrraacceess (Burnham 2012). The family are white British. Father's side is English, from the north of England, middle class and educated. Paternal grandfather died

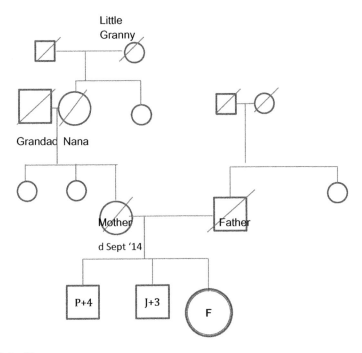

Fig. 3.1 F's genogram

before F was born. He was a headmaster. He was not a nice person. Paternal grandmother was also not a nice person. She died when F was about 6. Her death was not a loss to F, in fact, she remembered herself and her brothers being rather glad about it. F's father was a chemical engineer. He owned a number of properties. He was highly respected in the community.

The maternal side is from the northeast of England and working class. Mother's two sisters emigrated to other countries and F saw little or nothing of them growing up. She was close to her grandparents. Maternal grandfather died in the early 1980s. Maternal grandmother, Nana, was her saving grace, a loving and protective figure. They had a special relationship and she always felt safe with Nana, although she never told her what was happening at home. She was able to spend precious time with these grandparents. That relationship, especially the one with Nana, maybe at the core of her resilience to carry on. Just the mention of them brings a wistful smile.

Her mother had been an opera singer prior to marriage. She retrained as a teacher and eventually the headmistress of the primary school which her children attended.

There was intense marital discord and the mother descended into alcoholism dramatically during F's young childhood. She could not protect her daughter, though they became very close. F tried to become her protector, tried to make it better. It is unclear whether the mother actually knew what was happening in the lounge and in the bedrooms. Under pressure she sent F into those rooms: 'do it for me'. In addition to the direct abuse she suffered from the father, F was triangulated into the marital discord and became parentified in relation to her mother. She never ceased trying to 'make it better'. She still finds criticism of her mother very difficult if not impossible, continuing to protect and excuse her: still wanting to 'make it better.'

Theory box 3.2 The structural concepts of triangulation and parentification are relevant to an understanding of this dynamic (Minuchin 1974). The child in effect becomes the parent of the parent (Byng-Hall 1995) and takes on the responsibility for the parent's well-being. This is an inversion of the hierarchy. There may be times in children's lives when they need to become involved in the care of a parent. However in pathological parentification the demands go beyond the child's developmental capabilities and involve emotional caretaking, excessive and inappropriate demands which may not be explicitly stated, the child 'just knows', the expectation that the role will be permanent, compulsive caregiving (Bowlby and Crittenden), and leaves the child feeling responsible for the adult's emotional state and guilty when they are unable to make it better. In addition, the role is often a secret one, unacknowledged by the parent or by anyone else close in the family.

In attachment (Crittenden and Landini 2011) the child may come to see themselves as unlovable and idealise the parent. This was a strong theme in the early part of the work: 'there must be something wrong with me'.

The mental health implications for such a situation are profound. The Adverse Childhood Experiences (ACES) Research (Felitti et al. 1998) shows clearly how these very difficult and traumatic experiences in childhood have serious mental and physical health sequelae in later life.

It is not clear when the abuse started. As she became unable to speak when recalling events, it seemed to have started before she developed speech, when she was a pre-verbal child. The story has emerged over many sessions. There were months of working on the same issues, other months of dealing with current life dilemmas, still others where the work seemed to stall. The work is still emerging.

In brief, the father abused her on every level. He attacked her soul. He tried to steal her essence. He told her that her breathing was 'a waste of air'.

In addition to the sexual abuse from her father, she was gang-raped whilst walking home at the age of 16. This resulted in a pregnancy. She went north to stay with Little Nana and her great aunt during the pregnancy. No one spoke about it. She gave birth prematurely and had a glimpse at the baby boy before he was removed and given up for adoption. She does not know what happened to him. Each year she marks his birthday, some 30 odd years now. She wonders what happened to him, hopes he is well and happy. She is not yet ready to investigate.

Adolescence was turbulent, she became a weekly boarder, began to self-harm and developed an eating disorder which was untreated. Abuse continued and intensified. Sport was a positive outlet. She was skilled at hockey and football. She left home for university in the midlands, continuing to find relief in sport. He stalked her: sending her photographs of the flat where she lived, clearly having been outside, watching.

Theory box 3.3 Pauline Boss (2006), a systemic therapist, writes about the impact of ambiguous loss. The person is gone but they are not gone. The loss is never fully integrated. Closure is not possible. The baby that F carried but never met exists somewhere in an unknown world.

> The use of power in a coercive way undermines the target's sense of agency and autonomy. It was impossible to predict where he might turn up. Nowhere is safe. The person becomes an object, forever being watched, never private, the menace and the terror are inside the person.

She had tried therapy previously. She knew on some level that her survival depended on understanding and processing what had happened to her. Unfortunately, her first therapist fell in love with her and transgressed boundaries, expressing affection for her. That was highly unsafe and terrifying. After uncountable episodes of self-harm and several suicide attempts she found my colleague and began therapy in a safe and containing way with her. It was this colleague who brought her to the Surviving Spirits workshop where I had met her years before.

Getting Going

Although F wanted to be there and, once committed, was punctual and consistent, it was clear that talking itself was almost impossible. For the first few years she was accompanied by Bruiser, her stuffed toy dog who went with her to difficult situations. He was a source of strength (Fig. 3.2).

In the first year or so the sessions would start with her quickly becoming unable to speak, then getting angry with herself for her muteness. Her leg would start to move as if she were running. She would become very hot at the mention of 'father' or anything connected with her childhood experiences. We remembered that writing would work for her. So that was how we began: I would ask a question, she would right down an answer, often shaking and sweaty.

She wanted to put it all in a box. So by session three we had 4 boxes: 1 each for mother, father, self-hate and caring. Another slim box was added for 'space'. This contained F's Stanley knife which she gave me for safekeeping. Later two more boxes were added: one for her son whom she had seen once fleetingly when he was born, and one for her wife. Some of the boxes are pictured above with Bruiser.

Fig. 3.2 Bruiser with boxes

Although I tend to use action methods in my work, especially where verbalisation is difficult, I found it important for F to just be quite still and hold a containing presence. I introduced some action later. But very gently.

As F was going through some old papers at home she found a picture of herself around age 5. She brought it to a session, I found a frame and she has been with us ever since. At the end of each session she would write a short message for one of the boxes.

These boxes and the framed photo as well as her end of session message to one of the boxes became our reliable ritual.

A breakthrough came after about three months when F was able to find enough of her voice to tell me about her son and the rape. From then on her voice became stronger, her leg allowed her to speak and she became more articulate about the unspeakable things she had endured. She still became very hot when trying to process thoughts and feelings, and sometimes struggled to get the words out. However there has been steady and enduring progress.

In early sessions and sometimes even in later ones F would dissociate, simply leave the room in spirit, seem to shut down. At these times I would bring her back to the here and now, ground her in the room and in the therapeutic relationship and normalise this process as one of self-protection. She simply wasn't yet ready to go there yet and we would together make it safe enough to get her in and out of her experiences with her able to remain present.

Theory box 3.4 One of my main concerns was that of re-traumatisation. In the talking about it the danger is that it is relived again in an uncontained way that can cause further psychic damage. A lot of the early sessions focused on how she survived, the strengths and resilience that got her through. Her Nana was with us a great deal in those early sessions. Helping her to build a sense of personal agency was crucial. A great deal of reframing and beginning to change the meaning of events was important. Using the psychodramatic technique of the mirror position made it possible for her to look in on herself from the outside and realise that in fact she was not responsible for the abuse, nor had she done anything to deserve it. She was able to reflect on how she might intervene if she knew of this happening.

The Therapeutic Spiral Model (Hudgins 2002) teaches the importance of building the strengths to get into the trauma material with enough resilience to get out again without re-traumatising.

Containment was provided both in the session itself through the use of a candle burning in each session and the boxes themselves: a concrete representation of containment, thus adding to the creation of psychological space and safety. The importance of therapeutic ritual has long been acknowledged as a key factor in promoting healing (e.g. Imber-Black and Roberts 1992).

The field of interpersonal neurobiology which has gained ground in recent years helps psychotherapists across the board to understand the

---

internal body/brain system at work in helping to overcome trauma. Van der Kolk (2013) discusses the body/brain connection and the importance of the ability to dissociate. During traumatic experiences this ability keeps us safe. As therapists it is important to be able to help trauma survivors recognise and respect dissociation and help remove the need for it by creating safety. Porges (2017) speaks of the transformative power of feeling safe and describes the bi-directional communication between the body and the brain via the vagus nerve as important information. Smith (2013) in describing 'amygdala hijack' explains how trauma triggers (for F there were many) can trick the brain into thinking the trauma is happening now, the body responds with protective action. The person may not understand what is happening. The job of therapy is to make the person feel safe enough to begin to understand and put words to the 'nameless terror' that accompanies the feelings.

Stuff Happens

The therapy hadn't long started when her marriage began to run into difficulty. Not surprisingly F found sexual intimacy difficult. F had clearly confided in her wife about the abuse, but not the full extent of it. M, who had at first been understanding and sympathetic, eventually grew impatient that F was not able to 'get over it'. She demanded attention and thought her love and their loving relationship could 'cure' F and enable them to have a full sexual experience. This didn't happen; in fact it became more difficult for F, not less. She became highly avoidant and withdrew from M both physically and psychologically. The more M approached, the further F withdrew. This resulted in an escalation of unhappiness and despair and eventually brought about the end of the marriage.

This triggered a response in F which she experienced in childhood in relation to her mother, wishing to do something to make it better even in detriment to herself. I was concerned and offered to go with her to the lawyer. I acted as a sort of interpreter. She wanted to ensure M had a more than fair deal and felt she needed to compensate her for what she saw as her failure. My role in that sense was to help the lawyer understand that, unlike the divorce settlements I am used to hearing about, F wished to be overgenerous in her financial agreement and needed help to be more realistic in relation to what she herself needed.

Theory box 3.5 In attachment terms (Crittenden and Landini 2011) F has adopted a self-protective strategy in which she denigrates the self and idealises the 'other'. This strategy kept her alive in a situation which made no coherent sense. Believing that it must be your fault, you must deserve it somehow, there must be something wrong with you, enables the person to make a kind of sense of that which makes no sense at all.

These strategies once established can be carried into other significant relationships and emerge as patterns of relational interaction. F and M established an approach/avoidance pattern that is recognisable to many couple therapists (Watzlawick et al. 1967). Tomm et al. (2014) have gone further to identify patterns in interpersonal relationships which have a number of effects: both pathologising and therapeutic.

In year three of our work together F's mother became ill with a recurrence of pancreatic cancer. She had previously undergone a long and painful surgery. During that recovery F had been a diligent and faithful nurse to her. Now the cancer returned with vengeance and it quickly became apparent that she would not survive. She was given three months. She lived for 15, dying the day after F's birthday in 2014.

F moved out of her home and in with her mother and for the year and three months years did everything she could to make her mother's time meaningful and her life filled, whilst continuing to hold a demanding full-time job. She organised outings to the opera, ensured friends were able to visit and made the last months of her mother's life as pleasant and comfortable as possible. She reminded me that on hearing from the hospital that her father had died, her mother's response had been 'I'm free at last'. F felt deeply anguished for her mother that she would have so little time now left to enjoy life. She was determined to do everything she could to remedy that.

F continued therapy. The therapy at this time was focused on conversations she might have with her mother, questions she might try to get answered, questions she had held for a long time. Her protectiveness of her mother overruled her desire for answers. She just could not bring herself to ask the questions. Did she know what was happening? What kept her from taking F and leaving? Why could she not protect F? These questions went unanswered.

The funeral was attended by many. Her mother was loved in the community, having been a beloved headmistress and member of the amateur dramatic society and well known by many. F sang 'How Long Will I Love You' by Ellie Goulding at the funeral.

My 'Real Life Stuff'

Therapists too have a life outside of therapy. I would share some of what was going on in my family and work life. During our work together I obtained my doctorate in systemic psychotherapy, had a hip replacement, had a hysterectomy and follow up cancer treatment, became a grandmother, had children return to live with me, move out and move back in again, and fell down stairs dislocating my shoulder and needing surgery. True to her form F worries about me—and though I try to relieve her from that it is a mark of the importance of the relationship.

What's in the Box? The Progress of Therapy

Clearly therapy is not a linear process. It is start/stop, forward/backward, accelerator and brake. I will take each of the boxes in turn and, although they are all inter-related, I will focus on the main points in each. F labelled the boxes.

Caring—Wanting To, Seeking To, Needing To

This is the box of growing strength and resilience. We focused a lot on her circle of support, nurturance and friendship. Her Nana, who died in 2007 at the age of 98 was the main source of positive regard and hopeful caring. She was crucial to F's survival. Even though F was never able to talk to her about what was happening, her time with Nana was always positive. There were times when the father, mother and two brothers would go for exciting holidays abroad and F was left at home. She might have resented this but to spend two weeks in Nana's company without fear of abuse was the best time ever. Ever.

She described sleeping on a trundle next to Nana's bed with Grandad on the other side and Nana holding her hand until she went to sleep. Bliss.

At other times of danger at home she would creep into her brother's room and curl up like a puppy at the foot of his bed going to sleep there, hoping that would protect her. Sometimes it did.

A continual struggle in therapy was to connect her to her cognitive adult self to process these memories and feelings.

From this box, F's own voice says most of what needs saying. Here are a few excerpts from 'Caring: wanting to, seeking to, needing to.'

- Undated, I do come here every week And I have spoken about things I never thought I would. So, I guess I must care about me, oddly.
- Undated. [probably around the time of the divorce] Taking care of myself despite risking someone else being hurt.
- 19.10.12, I am talking and that is something I never thought I would do.
- 16.4.13, I think that some of what I have said or written recently is about me. That 'looking' at me is hard and some of it I haven't liked. Talking about what happened is different to looking at me, me inside.
- 25.4.13, If I could change one thing about the dream it would be that the 'little' me stood still, looked up, looked into the eyes of the 'violent' me and asked me to stop.

- 2.5.13, I cannot understand how a child can deserve that. It doesn't make sense. Were you so different? No, you were just a child. That wasn't your fault.
- 23.5.13, I love you Nana – always will, always. And I <u>know</u> you loved me and how grateful I am for that. My rock.
- 10.9.13, I love Bruiser's smell. It is all mine. He is my safe place ☺.
- 26.3.13, undo and step inside each other. To talk, to share, to laugh, to care.
- 22.8.13, You (little one) weren't able to make your own decisions – a young age and all that. You (not the little one) are.
- 31.10.13, 18,15,21,20,9,14,5. 9, 19. 7,15,15,4.
- 29.1.14, ◎------- How to unravel?.
- 30.4.14, Be your own person. Do not become someone PURELY because you are in a relationship. You can exist outside others. I think.

Theory box 3.6 These are unique and individual strength-building statements following best practice from Therapeutic Spiral (Hudgins 2002). See theory box 3.4 for a reference. Karl Tomm writes of ethical postures: opening space, therapeutic loving and increasing possibilities (in Freedman and Combs 1996).

<u>Self-hate.</u> What emerged over months and years is that F had almost fully taken on board her father's attack message and his description of her as 'a waste of air.' She has spent most of her life feeling unworthy of love (even though she has been loved by many), feeling like a fake and a fraud. If people really knew her it would be impossible for them to love her or even like her.

There are not many messages in the 'self-hate' box. Those that are there express shame and fear. F has been able to describe a childhood in which she was a 'really difficult child'. She was disobedient at school attending the school where her mother was headmistress. She was bullied and taunted by other children, there was an 'I hate F' club. She spat, kicked and punched her way through primary school and no one asked why this child was behaving this way. There was one episode of a visit by social services. Someone had reported bruises. She remembered the social worker sitting at her kitchen table and being convinced by her mother that everything was ok.

Meanwhile abuse continued and increased. Arguments between the parents increased. Mother's drinking increased. F just wanted to make it better for her mother at home. One response to mother's unhappiness was to clean the cupboards, hoping that would make her happy. That is the memory from age 8.

She felt she somehow deserved it. Everything: the bullying, the triangulation, the abuse.

The self-hate story increased in adolescence with her starting to 'carve up' her arms and legs. She hid this as much as possible. She also started denying herself food. Later she would deny comfort, sleeping on the floor, no duvet, no sheets.

Even though cognitively she is able to comprehend the problem with these thoughts and knows for sure what she would do as a teacher should a child present with these behaviours, she struggled to feel the injustice in her heart.

Writing has helped. She began in adolescence. It was a place she could at least get her feelings on to paper, even if they remained unseen for years. This is one which we chose together from many.

Caught

Caught inside with feelings that are numb
Shouting words of desperation that are silent
Holding tightly to visions of hope as if it is water
Hugging, clinging to people who are mere shadows
By F

Space

This box has just 8 messages. They are generally pleas for self-acceptance. It also contains Stanley, a retractable utility knife. I am keeping it safe. She has never asked for it. I have also checked regularly in the early stages that she had not replaced it and was not cutting.

Father

- Undated, About doing me a favour, loving me cos no one else will, being worthless, should b grateful, told me to say I wanted it, I wanted him to do what he did. Would list the things I had done wrong and say that each thing had to be punished.
- 11.9.12, Demands, expectations, knowing what was expected, what was about to happen, the triggers, the footsteps, the door closing, that sort of stuff.
- 19.10.12, When he used to say he would be unwell or it was dangerous for him to not be 'satisfied' if he was 'turned on' – I felt guilty and like I had let him down, worried he would be in a bad way because of me. Something felt like a kind of duty.
- 23.12.12, It's the things he didn't say – he never said what I should say, he said what I shouldn't say and he said that 'sport was rough'. I was the daughter of a successful man, do you know what that means and how much people respected him and the influence he has. Big and powerful man in the community. Small and worthless little voice of the daughter.
- 3.1.13, When he died I wanted to 'wake' him up – I knew he had the easy escape. I didn't care he had died, I'm not sure anyone did, but I felt angry that he wasn't alive anymore and I had missed my chance to tell him he made me sad. As for feelings now – I feel that little girl was cheated out of her smiles and innocence.

These are just a small sample of what's in the box. Most are from the time when she could not speak. She tried but the words would not come out. The break though came in a session where she deeply realised he was still controlling her, really felt it, not just intellectualised it. From then on she started getting her voice back (Fig. 3.3).

She used to speak about wanting to scour herself, scour him out. She would make a gesture like pulling it out of her. She has some full memories from her later childhood and adolescence. There are some fragments of memory from when she was very tiny, probably before speech had fully developed.

She has powerful sense memories, especially smell, but all of the others as well: taste, touch, sound, sight. All vivid. The colour red is hated and feared. Especially on a bathrobe. He body overheats, her leg would tap as if she was running.

Fig. 3.3   Containing and healing toxic messages

Abuse happened at home, in her bedroom, his bedroom, the lounge. It happened in cars and vans. She was taken to other places to be abused, other houses. He owned property. An email following a session 'Bath, at the house in XXXX. Old bath, old odd taps, some rust. Stand alone bath, weird feet on the bath. Smells damp in the room. Cold water - feels cold, maybe it isn't? Men. Smoking. Smells.'

He told her he was doing her a favour because no one would ever want her.

He invaded her dreams. We set up lucid dreaming. She was able to chase him out of her dreams, at least sometimes. She was proud of that and I was proud of her too.

Tired of Sleeping

A whole third of our lives, spent not here.
Seems a waste, seems a shame.
It's not reality, it's all a dream.
Reality, dreams, they're not the same.
Nightmares, it's all so frightening.
Staying awake can be a solution
No mad attacks, no loss of life
No being locked and tired in that institution
It's a strange thing, tiredness
Not there, then it starts creeping
Perhaps I'm just afraid of dreams
Or perhaps I'm just tired of sleeping.
By F

When she found it too much she might dissociate. This was obvious as she would seem to be somewhere else. She would come back we would reground, regroup and review. She wanted to continue even though it was hard. No one had heard the detail before. And there is more to come. We are definitely 'walking around in difficult moments!'

To say that this woman has resilience in the bucket loads is an understatement. If she didn't she would not be here. Somehow she managed to survive the attacks. Her ability to dissociate kept her core safe, he tried very hard but wasn't able to destroy her spirit.

Trying

> I attempt to hold onto the wonderful and
> loving things I have managed to discover
> within my desperate life.
> I try so hard to overpower the pain and
> Hurt with all the strength and power
> that others diffuse into me.
> I hold onto the feelings of today, the
> promises of tomorrow – in the hope that
> they bring warmer feelings inside.
> By F

During the most difficult disclosure days we would stay in touch between sessions.

I worried for her and sent thoughts: 'Came across this saying from Mahatma Ghandi. *"Prayer is not asking. It is a longing of the soul. It is daily admission of one's weakness. It is better in prayer to have a heart without words than words without a heart."*'

I sent quotes from Maya Angelou and others that are readily found and uplifting.

Theory box 3.7 The dynamics of abuse are redolent with shame, self-contempt and disgust. Memory. Dallos and Vetere (2009) write of walking around in difficult moments. With F there were many, and more to come. It was hard to stay in them, try to make sense, just be in the experiencing and hold the space as safely as possible. Each session ends with a (very safe but deeply held) hug. The physical contact has felt an important decontaminant. A wordless connection of shared openness. Many therapeutic repetitions of 'it's not your shame, it's his'. She struggled and continues to struggle to change the narrative. But the adversary is becoming weaker: love is winning. Resilience has been reconstructed from a social constructionist perspective by Gerrilyn Smith as 'a co-constructed emergent quality, rather than one which resides somewhere within an individual' (Smith 2013, p. 29).

Mother

This box is full of messages, mainly of love and missing her. She is always referred to as 'mother', never mum or mummy. If ever I make a mistake and refer to 'your mum', I get corrected: 'mother': said quietly but emphatically.

The work with mother seems to be split into three phases: when healthy, during her illness, and that following her death.

This is complex, much more complex than the work with her overt abuser. That has been relatively straightforward as she has no ambivalence in relation to him. It's not hard to be angry and revolted.

On the one hand she knows her mother not only failed to protect her but actively sent her into him, knowing what would happen.

> An undated message in the box: 'I remember times when we were together that she would say things like "please go and see your father, he will only take it out on me if you don't. Please. For me".
>
> … I wasn't a young child, what the fuck was I doing, feels like a weakness, like I almost allowed it, I am not proud of it. It is part of why I feel I deserved it'.

On the other hand, she became, in a strange and continual role reversal, her mother's protector and caretaker. As such she genuinely loved and cherished her. And clearly underwent enormous sacrifices for her. This began in childhood and continues up to now, almost 5 years after her death.

During her mother's illness we talked a lot about the questions she might ask.

- 6.3.14, <u>Mother</u>. Question: was there something I did when I was growing up that meant it was deserved? If not, then WHY?
- 18.6.14, You like jigsaws. The questions are just to enable the final jigsaw to be completed. Not about blame. Just about knowing.

She never did ask the questions: just concentrated on caring. F's mother died on 14.9.14, the day after F's birthday. She said she would hang on for that and she did.

When therapy faltered following the death of her mother F started missing sessions (always with notice). A meeting had to be attended, she was ill, she injured herself. These were of course real events but there seemed to be a lot of them. Sometimes there would be six week gaps. Sessions which did take place were filled with grief.

We reviewed therapy and I offered three explanations: we were stuck, she was avoiding something, or perhaps she'd done enough or as much as she could for the moment and we should pause or end therapy. The idea of finishing caused her to become overheated and a return of the struggle to speak. It became clear that her therapy was not over.

Messages to her mother from then on were full of fondness, grief and missing her. In understanding the hiccup to therapy she was able to say that she just could not bear to have her mother 'dissed'. By this I think she wanted to preserve the preciousness of the last few years post father. I understand this on a gut level, though struggle with it as a therapist, thinking it would help her to locate responsibility. F and I move on together.

Theory box 3.8 In attachment and narrative work, the process of developing a coherent narrative, one that makes sense of the person's experience is considered a core therapeutic aim (Dallos and Vetere 2009). For F the challenge was, and to some extent still is, being able to recognise her mother's responsibility for not protecting her and at the same time widening the lens to understand that apportioning blame in this instance is not therapeutically helpful. Honouring the relationship in which F has so much invested and deconstructing all its levels of complexity is our continuing therapeutic challenge. This involves lifting shame and increasing our understanding of that deep connection.

The Therapist's Story

What a journey: awe-inspiring and at times terrifying. There have been strong echoes of thinking and feeling between us. I have been proud of her and myself. I have felt like a useless therapist, not good enough, smart enough or intuitive enough, echoing some of her self-hatred. I have also known that I have held the space and made a safe container. Our dance is one of closeness and then some distance. She is forgiving when I get it wrong. I do make mistakes.

My hope is that F would say that she doesn't have to hide when she is here. That she can be her whole self. I know she still struggles with shame that does not belong to her. I will continue to try to help her to give it back where it does belong.

Thank goodness for good clear clinical consultation. I have been able to bring my successes and my misgivings, concerns and worries to that safe space without fear. F has also been curious about my consultant and has asked what and how I share information. I am able to share with my consultant without censoring, even when I feel anxious. This has felt like Karl Tomm's ideas of therapeutic loving: opening space (in Freedman and Combs 1996). I hope that part of the 'echo' we have together is that we both feel free to really bring ourselves into the therapy room.

I feel immensely privileged to have met F, to have been able to work with her and witness the emergence of her story which is still emerging. She is a part of my life and has a special place in my heart. Each session is an encounter in which we both feel alive and fully present.

Over these years I have developed both personally and professionally. Professionally I have deepened my knowledge of trauma work and attachment. Personally, in addition to the chronological events mentioned earlier, I have found a place in my heart for the lovely bright-eyed child inside the competent, complex, feisty and loving woman that F has become. She will always remain there. She has touched me in profound ways and that has altered how I can be in the for the better.

> **Theory box 3.9. The therapeutic relationship** The danger to the therapist in the therapeutic relationship such as this is the possibility of secondary traumatisation. There have been times when I have felt very worried and have carried the worry for some days. Smith identifies this as a 'trauma specific supervision issue' (2013, p. 149). Thankfully, as stated earlier, I have extremely helpful clinical consultation which as unfailingly helped when I have been in the doldrums about my own abilities as a therapist and has also helped me celebrate F's progress and achievements.
>
> Limbic resonance, a midbrain to midbrain phenomenon, is the capacity to share and synchronise deep emotional states. In attachment terms we feel understood. More than that we 'feel felt' on an emotional level. Lewis et al. (2000) identify limbic resonance as the source of empathy and mutual exchange.

Post Script

Jakob Moreno, who developed psychodrama along with his life partner, Zerka, wrote in 1914: Invitation to an Encounter

'A meeting of two:
Eye to eye, face to face.
And when you are near
I will tear your eyes out
And will place them instead of mine,
And you will tear my eyes out
And will place them instead of yours,
Then I will look at you
With your eyes
And you will look at me
With mine'.

References

Boss, P. (2006). *Loss, trauma and resilience: Therapeutic work with ambiguous loss.* New York: W. W. Norton.

Burnham, J. (2012). Developments in Social GRRRAAACCEEESSS: Visible-invisible and voiced-unvoiced. In I.-B. Kause (Ed.), *Culture and reflexivity in systemic psychotherapy: Mutual perspectives.* London: Karnac.

Byng-Hall, J. (1995). *Rewriting family scripts.* New York: Guilford.

Crittenden, P. M. (2008/2016). *Raising parents: Attachment, representation, and treatment* (2nd ed.). Abingdon, Oxon: Routledge.

Crittenden, P. M., & Landini, A. (2011). *Assessing adult attachment: A dynamic-maturational approach to discourse analysis.* New York: W. W. Norton.

Dallos, R., & Vetere, A. (2009). *Systemic therapy and attachment narratives.* London: Routledge.

Felitti, M. D., Anda, R. F., Nordenberg, M. D., et al (1998). Relationship of childhood abuse and household dysfunction to many of the leading causes of death in adults: The Adverse Childhood Experiences (ACE) Study. *American Journal of Preventative Medicine, 14,* 245–258.

Freedman, J., & Combs, G. (1996). *Narrative therapy: The social construction of preferred realities.* New York: W. W. Norton.

Hudgins, M. K. (2002). *Experiential treatment for PTSD: The therapeutic spiral model.* New York: Springer.

Imber-Black, E., & Roberts, J. (1992). *Rituals for our times.* New York: Harper Perennial.

Lewis, T., Amini, F., & Lannon, R. (2000). *A general theory of love.* New York: Random House.

McGoldrick, M., Gerson, R., & Petry, S. S. (2008). *Genograms: Assessment and intervention.* New York: W. W. Norton.

Minuchin, S. (1974). *Families and family therapy.* London: Tavistock Publications.

Moreno, J. L. (1914). *Einladung zu einer Begegnung* (Invitation to an encounter). Vienna.

Pearce, W. B. (2007). *Making social worlds: A communication perspective.* Malden, MA: Blackwell.

Pearce, K. (2012). *Compassionate Communicating Because Moments Matter.* Lulu.

Pearce, W. B., & Littlejohn, S. W. (1997). *Moral conflict: When social worlds collide.* Thousand Oaks, CA: Sage.

Porges, S. (2017). *The pocket guide to the polyvagal theory: The transformative power of feeling safe.* New York: W. W. Norton.

Smith, G. (2013). *Working with trauma: Systemic approaches.* New York: Palgrave Macmillan.

Tomm, K., St. George, S., Wulff, D., & Strong, T. (2014). *Patterns in interpersonal interactions: Inviting relational understandings for therapeutic change.* New York: Routledge.

van der Kolk, B. (2013). *The body keeps the score: Mind, brain and body in the transformation of trauma.* London, UK: Penguin Random House.

Watzlawick, P., Beavin Bavelas, J., & Jackson, D. (1967). *Pragmatics of human communication: A study of interactional patterns, pathologies and paradoxes.* New York: W. W. Norton.

4

And It Takes as Long as It Takes

Ros Draper

Introduction

Therapy whether long or short term is an evolving and collaborative process so to try and convey this process I invited three clients to join with me in writing this chapter. I have structured the chapter in sections aimed at providing the reader with an experience, despite being on a page, of the living dialogical process that is therapy.

While writing this piece I have realised that in addition to the well documented non-specific factors like a warm empathic relationship, attentive listening, and so on, that the prerequisites for any successful therapeutic relationship, long or short, are the more specific ideas and practices associated with systemic thinking. These are generic to all my work whether I am meeting with clients for a few weeks or over several

R. Draper (✉)
Petersfield, UK
e-mail: rosdraper@crisalida.co.uk

© The Author(s) 2020
A. Vetere and J. Sheehan (eds.), *Long Term Systemic Therapy*,
Palgrave Texts in Counselling and Psychotherapy,
https://doi.org/10.1007/978-3-030-44511-9_4

years. So I would claim that systemic ideas and practices lend themselves equally well to short or long term therapeutic interventions.

Having many years of experience working in the public and voluntary sector, at present I work only in independent practice with individuals, couples and families—sometimes over time, over many stages of the life cycle, so often over three or four generations. My hope is that the aspects of my work described in this chapter will be of use to professionals working in contexts where the therapy resource offered to clients can be time limited. When beginning a relationship with clients my practice is to say I take seriously my responsibility to ensure our meetings are making a difference in their lives. So when agreeing on an initial contract of up to 8 sessions I explain the importance of reviewing together the progress, or not, of the work and say that as the work proceeds I will regularly be asking them for feedback.

Beginnings and Endings

In what some see as contrary I speak at the beginning about the end and letting clients know that I am confident they will know when the time comes to finish the work. Including this at an early stage comes from my belief that an important part of healing is creating a shared recognition with clients that they are the experts about themselves and not me as the therapist. Another reason to introduce endings at the beginning is that the making of better and 'good enough' endings for people who have experienced the trauma of abrupt, unplanned and wounding endings and losses in their lives is I believe a major part of the therapeutic process. The reader will also I am sure recognise that the distress associated with unplanned and unpredictable losses and endings is frequently what drives people to seek therapy in the first place. My intention therefore is early on in therapy to convey my recognition that clients need and indeed are entitled to feel in charge of the ending process, to experience this ending differently and as a collaborative process.

The chapter title comes directly from my memories of questioning myself and my supervisor about whether what was happening in particular therapeutic relationships was 'ok' since while the work seemed to be making a difference for the clients there was as yet no end in sight. Also the clients themselves were clear there were still changes they wanted to make in their lives and experienced our conversations as useful. Supervision bringing an alternative lens is an invaluable therapeutic resource as well as a check on whether collaborative working is at risk of becoming too cosy and comfortable.

What follows is a description of how I have structured the chapter to include clients' voices and what I am hoping the structure will provide for the reader. Then I describe some of the systemic, ideas and practices interwoven with other ideas that inform how I show up when meeting with clients.

The next section of the chapter consists of three clients' responses to what I have written. I invite the clients to offer their reflections on what I have written paying particular attention both to what does and what does not resonate and make sense to them based on their experiences of our work together. In addition I ask them to let me know what they feel from their reading I may have omitted in what I have written and which they think is an important aspect of their experience in therapy that they would like emphasised.

What particularly interests me given the importance of allowing feedback to inform my practice (Miller et al. 2016) is the extent to which clients' experience of therapy does, or maybe more importantly does not, resonate with the ideas and practices I claim influence my practice.

In continuing I offer some reflections and responses to clients' feedback. In conclusion, I then invite the clients who have generously agreed to collaborate with me in writing this chapter to read my responses to their reflections and offer any further observations they have and wish to share with me and the reader......in effect to have the last word.

To preserve a flow in my narrative, the originators of ideas and practices are identified in brackets as we go along with more detailed references at end of the chapter.

With this structure in mind, my hope is that the reader will have an experience of firstly witnessing a reflecting process (Andersen 1987) and as they read hopefully find some of what they read of interest and relevant to their own practice Secondly I hope the reader will notice as they read how what comes up in their own inner dialogue—their 'reflection in action' (Schon 1983) puts them in touch with their own self reflexivity and creativity as professionals.

I start from a position of believing transformational change by which I mean things will never be the same again (Bateson 1990; Selvini Palazolli et al. 1978) is possible. So my first job is to offer clients a safe welcoming 'potential space' (Winnicott 1965), presence, responsiveness to feedback, compassion (Gilbert 2009) and acceptance (Rogers 1957). These are some of the necessary conditions if clients are to speak the unspeakable in my presence as therapist and witness.

It is such a relational space in which the therapist's attentive presence can validate and affirm clients stories as well as embody responsiveness to feedback that does I believe invite clients into a dialogic process. Winnicott's 'potential space', can for clients compensate for missed, distorted or damaging experiences of the safe relational space in which resilience develops. I emphasise with clients that it is the experience of the collaborative relational space co-created by clients and therapist that is healing, can contribute to restoring resilience and developing awareness not the therapist.

However when people first show up in my consulting room I also have in my head that implicit in their appearing, along with their courage, is their ambivalence about the challenges involved when contemplating change—well articulated as: 'please take away my pain but don't you dare ask me to change'.

So when trying to interest clients in moving beyond the inevitable 'stuckness' of living with this contradiction and to risk contemplating changing unwanted behaviour patterns I have found the following ideas from the building trade can be useful:

Removal: to take away or abolish what is unwanted
Restoration: to give back that which was lost
Renovation: to repair something broken sometimes adding new elements
Remodel: to reorganise, reshape, alter or renew.

Analogies and metaphors are useful particularly when trying to talk about change so that the risks involved when contemplating change seem less frightening for clients.

When as clients sometimes say 'I want or wish things could be as they were' builders' speak can be useful: 'If your goal is to make your building (person) look like the original structure, then restoration is definitely right for you. However, be prepared to still do some renovation and remodelling, as some parts may not be able to be fully restored'. So if as often happens during therapy clients accept and embrace the fact that things can never be the same again, I then frequently hear: 'I now feel more like my real authentic self than I have ever felt and am certainly more myself than when we started working together'.

Human beings are of course very different from buildings but the process of renewing or repairing a building or structure by replacing the old with the new and in some cases adding new components has a certain resonance about it when I think of what might be a good outcome of therapy: the collaboration has successfully enabled clients 'reconnection' to themselves and their significant others thus enabling a redefinition of their relationships (Bateson 1972) with themselves and their significant others.

Since we also frequently speak of people being 'restored' to good health and wellbeing the analogy of a plant can be useful too when introducing ideas about recovery, healing and change. For me, the plant analogy resonates particularly with the systemic idea that within all living systems there is a drive towards health (Maturana and Varela 1980).

Plants like everything else in the natural world including human beings have a drive for survival...it is in our DNA...the way we are made. So human beings like plants while they can adapt to adversity and survive are not being the best version of themselves they can be. With plants this can be because of lack of sunlight, poor quality or toxic soil, not enough water or space to grow, etc. More often than not clients easily identify with this analogy offering their own ideas about what has stunted and/or is hindering their growth and what they need to become a flourishing 'plant' again......the version of themselves they long to be.

Given all behaviour is a communication and we cannot not communicate (Watzlawick et al. 1967) conveying to clients that there is an emotional logic to symptoms, disturbing and distressing behaviour patterns they may be experiencing is an idea that informs all my work. Therefore developing with clients a shared recognition and understanding— what I think of as a coherent (Bowlby 1988) or positive connotation (Selvini Palazolli et al. 1978) narrative—about what makes symptoms and unwanted behaviours such vital and necessary parts of their survival kit is for me a core relational process in therapy (Ecker et al. 2012). My experience is that the affirmation of such an emotional logic can in time become the springboard for clients developing self-compassion (Neff 2010) as well as providing the all-important leverage for change.

At some stage in a therapeutic relationship, I will also want to be conveying that feelings don't kill people but the chronic lingering toxicity of internal conflict due to suppression and/or denial of scary feelings is bad for our health. Banishing conflictual feelings to the unconscious for purposes of self-protection during early years, while making sense at the level of attempts at self-protection, usually proves to be damaging to our emotional, physical, spiritual wellbeing in later life.

Such recognition and shared understanding between clients and therapists can often lead to uncovering clients' awareness of their 'resistance' to change. Reframing such 'resistance' as another important aspect of their survival kit and response to intentional or unintentional neglect and/or abuse, or other traumatic childhood events (see the ACE study Adverse Childhood Experiences 1998) has become for me an important building block in normalising, as opposed to pathologising, adaptive symptom generating behaviour patterns (Crittenden 2000).

I am also curious to understand what is a client's relationship with change. Often asking such a question at first flummoxes clients but is crucial if promoting change is to be at the centre of any therapeutic relationship. How clients respond to the question reveals how hopeful or not they are about what change is possible. As clients explore the relevance of the question, often disappointment, hopelessness as well as more ambivalence surfaces. While trying to convey acceptance of whatever clients entrust to me of their internal worlds I sometimes explicitly offer to hold for them, if they wish, the hope of change until such time as they can hold it for themselves. After all holding hope themselves means clients must be ready to risk believing that ridding themselves of the distresses and disturbances they are experiencing is not only something they want but definitely also possible.

As therapy progresses it is usually necessary to revisit wounding experiences in clients' lives. Often no more than a sideways glance is possible to begin with since the pain anticipated by the clients should they revisit those episodes in their story can seem intolerable. But an acknowledgement and naming of neglect and/or abuse with an agreement between clients and therapist that even if 'parked' for the time being these are core issues relevant to and maintaining present unwanted behaviour patterns and will need unpicking is for me central to our collaboration.

Typically clients say there is relief in naming intense unwanted, sometimes horrifying, usually but not exclusively, family of origin experiences. Only with the validating experience of being heard can clients allow themselves to own the connections between early trauma and their present unwanted and disturbing feelings and the behaviour patterns that negatively impact current relationships as well as how they view themselves. There is a to-ing and fro-ing between memories stored in the limbic system (felt experiences) and cognitive processes (in the neo cortex) as clients make new meanings of how early wounding experiences are contributing to their current unwanted behaviours and distress. Once the connections are made there is space for the inevitable anger and grief and eventually something new to emerge. Frequently to clients' surprise at first, I suggest what needs to emerge is their own awareness and recognition of the legitimacy of their unfulfilled longings to have had their childhood needs met by the adults who were responsible for their care and safety.

As regrets and grief about the losses of what might have been for clients in their earlier years are acknowledged and examined frequently with tears, clients also begin to develop or restore their capacity for discernment, self-regulation (Shore 2015) and reflective functioning about what it is they need in the present and from whom. It is when clients are able to name what they need in the present to keep themselves safe as well as to ensure their future wellbeing and flourishing, that how they need to change their own behaviour patterns becomes clear and can be understood. These behaviour changes can be both in their relationship with themselves or their relationships with significant others.

It is particularly in these later stages of therapy that '… it takes as long as it takes.' There is no orderly linear path rather a series of spirals, adaptations, trial and error learnings and improvisations (Bateson 1990) as clients reorganise the jigsaw pieces of their stories. Stories that now can begin to celebrate their courage, resilience and changes achieved while simultaneously being in and responding to the frequently unpredictable demands of their lives in the present. As a therapist it is when clients' begin to look forward, albeit sometimes with tentative confidence in their capacity for self care, that signals a more than 'good enough' outcome of the collaboration between clients and therapist.

The three clients with each of whom I have worked for over 3 years either weekly or fortnightly and then at diminishing intervals have chosen pseudonyms. In addition to asking for their responses to what I have written I also asked each of them to write an introductory sentence about their reasons for seeking therapy.

The three texts of their reflections appear here unedited and in alphabetical order according to pseudonym and with their agreement to publication.

———

AVA: '*I DID NOT HAVE CLEAR HOPES, MAYBE JUST A THOUGHT THAT IN THERAPY I MIGHT BE HEARD, THAT THERE MIGHT BE A SAFE PLACE TO VISIT THE DARKNESS AND TRAUMA INSIDE ME SO THAT I WAS NO LONGER HAUNTED BY ITS PRESENCE.*'

REMOVAL

To be asked to question whether I needed to hold onto a view, belief or behaviour that is damaging was a revelation. And when my position seemed intractable, to be able to honestly evaluate why I continued to hold onto something—even though I knew it was harming me—conversely created a space for change. I can either see the purpose it is still serving in my life and thus not berate myself that it is so hard to let go, or perhaps there will be that moment of clarity, the realisation that it no longer serves a function for me.

And slowly, there is freedom and the scope to change. Wherever I find myself, this is a non-judgemental process. There is no guilt that I have not yet moved from my position, instead there is a discussion of what might give me leverage to move forwards.

RESTORATION

For me, it is not the restoration of something that was lost that is most impor-tant, it is the acknowledgement, acceptance and mourning of the loss. To believe that as a child I had the right to protection by my parents, to be loved unconditionally for being me, to not be made to believe that I was bad. To know that this was my right has helped to heal the pain that it was not given. It allows me to grieve for what was lost, for the little girl inside me to have her pain acknowledged, and cry her tears.

To be shown that I do not need to feel bad that I craved something that is the right of every child has helped me to let go of some of the distress. I can now accept that the little girl I once was, did not receive everything she needed. Yes, this hurts, but not as much as the hole inside me when I lacked the understanding of what I missed. This is what has allowed restoration for me.

The change then comes with the awareness that although I still crave these things as an adult, it is now within my capacity to make them for myself. I have been able to understand that, as a child, your care-givers are your val-idators and to grow up in an environment where you are constantly invali-dated creates so much doubt. But the next stage of the journey is to build this validation for myself.

AUTHENTICITY

Restoration for me is a 'felt' entity. The 'before' me is an ephemeral idea but my restoration has come from my felt experience. To be authentic is about a sense of connectivity within myself. The trust built up in therapy first allowed me to understand and feel this authenticity and it is this that brings me to the 'real me'. I do not need to search for who I was before because I now know the lived experience of what it means to be me.

RECONNECTION

I had lost all sense of self. I had grown so used to denying my feelings that I no longer believed any of my emotions were real. Somewhere inside I knew that the things happening to me were bad but I thought it must be ok. The people I looked to for protection would not see and so l learnt to deny it to myself. To reconnect with my emotions was frightening. It meant a journey through the pain. But with therapy I learnt the most important lesson—pain can be travelled through and, to reach the other side, it's a journey that must be taken. I could spend my life avoiding feeling, to keep running from the pain. But then there would be no chance of happiness, a void without emotion.

To reconnect with significant figures in your life is a difficult part of the process. When these people have been the cause of the damage it is also about learning to let go of the connections that are harmful. For me, one of the most important parts of therapy has been learning that I do not need to rely on others to know that I am ok. It is a work in progress but to be able to feel whole, without the validation of those—who in theory you should have been able to feel the most connected to—is the greatest gift and strength.

The very beginnings of self-validation started when I was first listened to during therapy. My truth and voice were heard for the first time. And I was believed. It is many steps from here to self-validation, but until I was given the space to speak the unspeakable my journey could not begin.

ADAPTIVE SYMPTOM GENERATING BEHAVIOURS

To find that I was not crazy, mad or bad was transformational. Understanding the logic to my patterns of behaviour, my mental health struggles and embedded damaging beliefs, has given me the leverage to be able to move forwards and change. To comprehend that my self-harming behaviour allowed me to survive in a disordered world has removed the self-blame and the idea that I was simply 'crazy' as I had been told. As a child I needed to survive, but as an adult, removed from the situation, this understanding has created a platform for change and growth. If you have grown up in toxic soil then your growth is stunted and you adapt in any way needed to survive. This idea of a logical self-preservation has been a source of strength for me. I may have developed harmful ways of coping but I was still trying to survive. There must have been a little flame alive inside me, even in the darkest of days— an inner knowledge that, despite what the world around me was saying, this wasn't right. In recovery, this knowledge has been fed and thus the plant begins to grow, to find its place in the light again and flourish.

REVISITING THE PAST

To revisit the past was at first all about the felt experience—the fear, grief and anger. It was important to be heard, to have somewhere safe to open Pandora's box. To risk doing this, I needed to believe that there would be the time to process and deal with the darkness inside me. So many times in the past I had been asked to open the box only to be left with the overwhelming thoughts and feelings and no capacity to cope with them. But now, gradually, I am able to recognise what is my felt experience—to realise when I am being triggered into past feelings, thrown back into my primitive mind. I have learnt to understand these intense thoughts and emotions and make the connection between their cause and the damaging beliefs or behaviours they precipitate. To begin with, it was only a nascent awareness, I was able to say to myself, 'it is happening again, I am being triggered'. But now I am also learning that I have the capacity to interrupt my patterns of thought and response. If I can move from the raw emotional part of my mind to the analytical, then the past will no longer control me and I will not have to fear the darkness left behind.

ENDINGS

I did not know there could be good endings. They have always been painful, tearing me apart and leaving me more vulnerable than before. To know that I can be in control of the end, to be entrusted with having the wisdom and self-awareness to know when I am ready is empowering. How do you risk exposing your deepest vulnerabilities if you do not truly believe you will be given the time to heal? Recovery is not a single road. Growing up, in order to protect myself from further pain, I shut down my life. The world became very small and quiet. As I heal and realise my capacity for change, the walls I carefully built are tumbling down. Sometimes what is revealed is so very beautiful—new life and opportunities. But at other times, the falling bricks will unearth my vulnerabilities and the darkness will come close again. To know that 'it takes as long as it takes', that there is still the support for me to learn, gives me the courage to keep exploring and finding my place in the world once again.

———

KATHERINE: *FINDING LIFE AS A SINGLE PARENT ENOR-MOUSLY CHALLENGING AND STRUGGLING WITH THE*

IMPACT OF SEPARATION AND DIVORCE ON ALL THREE OF MY CHILDREN, PARTICULARLY MY YOUNGEST SON AGED FIVE YEARS, AS WELL AS ON MYSELF. I SOUGHT THERAPY TO HELP ME SUPPORT MY CHILDREN.

ENDINGS
I think this was very clear at the beginning though less overt as time went on—when I felt the need to pull away and that possibly therapy 'should' be finishing, I was aware that you did not always agree with my assessment—completely correctly as it inevitably transpired. The desire to 'end' therapy, to reach a sense of having completed something was, of course, part and parcel of the problem and when, in response to my expressed desire you gently suggested reducing session frequency as an initial step, it quickly became clear that there was still work to be done. Naturally, I did struggle with how long it was taking or rather why couldn't I do this fast, quicker, better! When the end it come it was clear, clean and without attached 'shoulds'.

...WHETHER COLLABORATIVE WORKING IS AT RISK OF BECOMING TOO COSY AND COMFORTABLE
For whom! I guess the judgment is between whether you are truly helping or enabling the situation to continue unresolved. In my case, and obviously with the benefit of hindsight, the time was essential. And maybe cosy and comfortable was also part of that. The tension between wanting to no longer need therapy and the desire to risk being truly seen (or change?) is a real challenge.

'WHEN I ACCEPT MYSELF JUST AS I AM THEN I CAN BEGIN TO CHANGE'
Took me several years to even voice the fear that change is not possible—the belief that 'people can't change fundamentally' which was, of course, my mother's position. The paradox was that I wanted to change to make myself more acceptable to those who sought to reject me because I believed their assertions (overt and implicit) that I was at fault while at the same time I held the belief that people don't change! Obviously a classic double bind—you have to change to be acceptable, you can't change. With a side order of loss of self along the way!

THE COLLABORATIVE RELATIONAL SPACE IS WHAT IS HEALING…AND NOT THE THERAPIST

I like this and it resonates—while I did feel the desire to please you, it never tipped into a real need and therefore avoided replicating other relationships.

BUT DON'T YOU DARE ASK ME TO CHANGE

Don't you dare ask me to change more—I'm lost already!

For me, my motivation for therapy was to help my son who was struggling. However, it also formed part of my long term 'self-improvement' programme—to make me tolerable to others when I've already tried everything and I'm without hope.

Please fix me so my family and friends can tolerate me but don't ask me to judge them or demand changes from them. They're right, they must be because no one has ever said otherwise, it's heretical to think otherwise and I'm a bad person because I do.

But I've already bent myself out of shape trying to do this and I'm losing myself. My family think I'm not good enough as I am, are you the same and will I be expected to give up the little bit of me I've managed to hang on to in order to make these changes? Obviously with the benefit of hindsight, what I was being asked to examine was my belief systems underlying my behaviour etc. but that's a moot point when you feel that it's you that is fundamentally unacceptable.

REMOVAL RESTORATION RENOVATION REMODEL

This doesn't particularly resonate but I suspect that was because you looked to help me identify how in my own professional practice as a complementary medicine practitioner I did already have a 'theory of change' so that ideas about change were already grounded in my own lived experiences with my patients.*

… WITH PLANTS THIS CAN BE BECAUSE OF LACK OF SUNLIGHT, POOR QUALITY OR TOXIC SOIL, NOT ENOUGH WATER OR SPACE TO GROW, ETC.

Again don't remember but see above*

WHEN AS CLIENTS SOMETIMES SAY 'I WANT OR WISH THINGS COULD BE AS THEY WERE'

You very much acknowledged my frustration with this and also the fact that things were not as I would like them to be. I felt that acknowledging hating things meant that life was not worth living but, by frequently acknowledging that I hated being a single parent, for example, you allowed me to see that I can hate a situation but that that doesn't define my life i.e. that it's safe to state a truth and that truth doesn't have to define me.

COHERENT NARRATIVE

I think that, ultimately, this is what has been transformative for me both for myself and in my dealings with others. In writing that, I am mindful that I'm not yet able to apply it to my parents even if intellectually I know it must be true! What has surprised me is the specificity of the words—the right words resonate like nothing else.

…LINGERING TOXICITY OF INTERNAL CONFLICT DUE TO SUPPRESSION AND/OR DENIAL OF SCARY FEELINGS…

This is something I did already know prior to starting therapy with you but the taboos surrounding my story did make me feel I would be struck down should I even dare to think about what my childhood was really like. 'Verboten' forbidden figured quite a lot around this.

REFRAMING SUCH 'RESISTANCE' AS ANOTHER IMPORTANT PART OF THEIR SURVIVAL KIT….

Reframing was something you used a lot and I still find it helpful

I AM THEN CURIOUS TO UNDERSTAND WHAT IS CLIENT'S RELATIONSHIP WITH CHANGE

Don't you dare ask me to change more—I'm lost already

…OFTEN DISAPPOINTMENT HOPELESSNESS AS WELL AS MORE AMBIVALENCE SURFACE

Absolutely, together with anger—I've changed myself so much in relation to my family and it's not enough. What other changes could possibly make a difference. I think I saw it as changing my behaviour, thinking, etc. so that I would be loved and yet I knew that was impossible without completely surrendering myself. I wanted the former but wasn't prepared to give up the latter, which is why I clung to the belief about change not being possible. Ultimately, however, what I was seeking was a way to be loved and still be me and I knew that was impossible. And absolutely you held the hope of change for me during this period while I tried, and failed, to find a way to sort this without looking at the reality of what was in front of me!

IF WE DO NOT TRANSFORM OUR PAIN WE WILL TRANSMIT IT

I don't remember you using this with me but then I arrived anxious about my son and seeking therapy to help support him—I was already aware of mitigating the impact of my upbringing on my children.

REVISIT WOUNDING EPISODES

It's challenging because it can be cathartic to revisit such old wounds but intolerable to look at the behaviour surrounding them and the detail.

...NAMING INTENSE UNWANTED, SOMETIMES HORRIFYING, USUALLY BUT NOT EXCLUSIVELY, FAMILY OF ORIGIN EXPERIENCES

I struggled with naming the behaviour. Even with you naming it still it felt heretical to even talk about some things! I noticed that you started with very gentle statements: 'their behaviour was not good', 'you did not get what you needed/deserved', through depersonalised statements: 'when people have experienced ...' etc. for a long period of time..., before making more overt statements and ultimately statements of fact 'Their behaviour was abusive'. I noticed each increase in statement strength and it was never comfortable but it was necessary.

...HOW THEY NEED TO CHANGE THEIR OWN BEHAVIOUR PATTERNS TO ENSURE THEIR WELLBEING AND FLOURISHING IN PRESENT DAY RELATIONSHIPS INCLUDING THEIR RELATIONSHIP WITH THEMSELVES

Absolutely! Without the process above, I'd never have got to recognising behaviour for what it is. When I started therapy, effectively I was looking for ways to change myself to enable me to tolerate more abuse. I'm now much clearer about my boundaries, where my responsibilities start and end and I now have the capacity for true choices in the way I interact with the people in my life, even if exercising those choices is still a work in progress!

...WHEN CLIENTS BEGIN TO LOOK FORWARD, ALBEIT SOMETIMES WITH TENTATIVE CONFIDENCE IN THEIR CAPACITY FOR SELF CARE, THAT SIGNALS A MORE THAN 'GOOD ENOUGH' OUTCOME OF THE COLLABORATION BETWEEN CLIENT AND THERAPIST.

Uncovering the belief that I was inherently intolerable and there was nothing I could do to change that led to the rapid unravelling and reframing of my position in the last few months of therapy. But to get there took a huge amount of work and time. Ultimately, looking back, the fact that you didn't give up on me, held on to the hope of change for me and saw me as worth continuing with even when it appeared that little progress was being made was what allowed me, eventually, to identify this belief, buried as it was under so many other unhelpful and restrictive beliefs. Once this belief had surfaced, everything else became simple and remarkably straightforward, no doubt due to the work we'd done. But the sticking with it when things didn't seem to be changing, the sense that you knew where we were going together with the idea that 'it takes as long as it takes' is what allowed me to get there.

My fear that I would have to change fundamentally has been realised and it's so simple and yet so profound at the same time—I have had to renew my relationship with myself, with my own truth, knowledge and power. I have embraced myself and my inner knowing and I have a sense of where my responsibilities in relationship to others start and end. I now have real choice in how I relate to myself, the rest of the world, how I view the behaviour of others and how I respond.

———

SARAH: *'THE IMPETUS FOR EMBARKING UPON THERAPY WITH ROS WAS THE DEATH OF MY MOTHER SEVERAL MONTHS EARLIER AND HOW THAT HAD LEFT ME FEELING.'*

ENDINGS

- *I found it helpful to discuss 'endings' at the start of the therapeutic relationship*

- *When ending the therapeutic relationship it was important to me to have a 'planned ending' particularly after the trauma of losing most of the important people in my life suddenly and unexpectedly.*

POTENTIAL SPACE

- *The collaborative relational space—was healing for me*
- *Ros was positive and encouraging that change could be achieved e.g. neuroscience*
- *Very much a collaborative journey towards healing.*

AMBIVALENT ABOUT CHANGE

- *For me, I don't believe that this was the case. I was seeking change. I was aware that what I was doing was not making me happy and I had a desire to 'thrive not just survive' but I didn't know how to achieve positive change. I felt as though I had come as far as I could on my own and now needed the assistance of an 'expert'. However I have previously had significant experience of therapy and also undertaken a twelve step programme with an emphasis on change and acceptance.*

AUTHENTIC SELF

- *I feel that there was a need for me to 'discover' my true self/my authentic self rather than 'restore' as I feel I never knew her/was aware of her before.*
- *Couldn't really envisage what a flourishing Sarah would look like or what I would need to become flourishing—have always had difficulty knowing what I want or what I need. Much easier to identify what I don't want/need!*

COHERENT NARRATIVE

- *Helpful to look at my 'symptoms'/unwanted behaviours as part of my 'survival kit' and how they had previously been helpful but were now no longer needed. Comforting to know that they were there for a reason not just because there was something 'wrong' with me/bad person etc.*

- *I was feeling 'toxic' and ill at ease due to my thoughts and feelings. Dissatisfied with myself and my relationships with others*
- *Reflecting back—I had a huge need to cultivate some self-compassion and forgive myself*
    I had a need to be heard and to make the connection between childhood hurt and unwanted feelings and unhelpful patterns of behaviour. Strong feelings of not being heard as a child continued into adulthood—not getting my needs met
- *Through this process there were a lot of tears and grief for my early years*
- *Through this process came a realisation of what I needed to change in order to thrive*
- *Key components towards healing: courage, resilience and change*
- *Therapy has been like shedding layers of hard calloused skin which were both protective but were also causing pain and discomfort. I have emerged from within—bright and shiny. The process has been transformative. I now have compassion for myself and the freedom to choose positive relationships with others.*

———————

Working out how best to convey my responses to these reflections has involved reading and rereading what Ava, Katherine and Sarah have offered. Typical of any reflecting process on my first reading I was aware of my attention being drawn to the content and of being moved as I read by the extent each has been willing to share of themselves.

What stood out for me as I read the reflections is the way each person describes how reclaiming agency of themselves and of their relationships is integral to their journey in therapy. I like to think that this has been in part accomplished by gently insisting that each client uncover the wisdom and expertise they already have about themselves. As I see it the work in therapy is primarily about creating conditions and holding a safe space in which as clients develop a curiosity about troubling aspects of their stories they recognise their own capacity for re editing their family stories (Byng Hall 1979). It is during such explorations that new possibilities clients can own become visible. It is the careful collaborative deconstruction of unwanted behaviour patterns that opens up space for alternatives to emerge.

Then on second and subsequent readings my curiosity focussed on what are the themes common to each piece of writing, what themes seem to me to have greater emphasis in each person's account and what reflections do I think could be useful for the reader given the subject of this book.

That Ava, Katherine and Sarah mention nothing explicitly about what they feel I have omitted or that they want emphasised more I see as an example of the need always to expect there to be unintended consequences any time as systemic practitioners we intervene in a system. My intervention in this instance was my request to them to read and offer reflections on the first section of this chapter that included identifying what they felt from their reading I may have omitted and/or what needed more emphasis in what I have written.

So I decided my reflections here on what they have shared could be in two sections. Firstly I focus on what I see as common threads in all three accounts. Then I offer some thoughts on some themes that it seems to me Ava, Katherine and Sarah individually emphasise.

The themes I see as common to each account in alphabetical order are: being heard, coherent narrative, collaborative working, endings, grief, it takes as long as it takes, potential space, revisiting the past, restoration, survival kit, time to process what comes up.

The fact that all three writers in their reflections mention the importance for their healing of being heard, endings, it takes as long as it takes and time to process what comes up beautifully supports the editors' purposes in bringing this book into being.

The reader might say these themes are common to psychotherapy in general and not the exclusive domain of systemic practice and I would agree. What I believe can be distinctively systemic is the way systemic practitioners work with these themes.

Some of the distinctive hallmarks of systemic thinking and practice are that we ask many different kinds of questions (Tomm 1988), give attention to the contexts in which feelings, relationships and behaviour happen, stay closely connected to feedback, are intentional when inviting clients to consider new connections in their stories, attempt to open up spaces for the emergence of new meanings and options for action by wondering and thinking out loud about what clients are sharing. In my own thinking all these practices connect to my emphasis on client as expert and conversely therapist as naïve ignorant explorer—like a Colombo or a Sherlock Holmes according to your preference!

Among the other themes common to what Ava, Katherine and Sarah have written I link collaborative working with potential space since one implies the other. My approach to revisiting the past focuses on how clients' remember their relationships with significant adults at different stages in the life cycle and how challenges and/or discomforts in clients' present-day relationships across the generations reflect relationship patterns developed at earlier times. All three writers have mentioned the significant part grief plays when revisiting the past. Mingled with the pain of grieving the losses of what might have been can for clients be relief when their unmet needs and yearning for unconditional love and acceptance are affirmed as an aspect of their humanity and not something bad, mad or shameful.

Survival kit and coherent narrative also go together as the self-compassion necessary for there to be a coherent story requires clients to develop an understanding of how any truly coherent and liveable with narrative they create will validate their survival strategies.

The different ways Ava, Katherine and Sarah reflect on how they related to my restoration metaphor is a good example of what can happen when an idea offered seems not to be such a good fit. Each of them shared some really important aspects of their journey as they described how reflecting on restoration put them in touch with aspects of their experience in therapy that have particular relevance to their reconnecting with themselves.

So if as a therapist I find what clients say does not for me immediately connect with an idea I might have been offering, I remind myself that 'all behaviour is feedback'. Then I can hear whatever clients are saying as the way they are responding to what I have offered so I just need to wait for the connections to become clearer. Waiting allied as it is with presence has its rewards in therapy as does reminding myself that I only say what clients hear.

———

Conclusion

What follows are my reflections on some of the themes which seem to have a particular emphasis in what Ava, Katherine and Sarah have written. I am of course aware that my own prejudices (Cecchin et al. 1994) govern which themes I have chosen as a focus for the reflections I offer here.

AVA
'to be asked to question whether I needed to hold onto a view, belief or behaviour that is damaging was a revelation' Central to my systemic practice is developing conversations in which clients see clearly the links between their beliefs and behaviour. This understanding then provides the safe platform from which clients can risk becoming observers to their own process and reflecting on the question to which Ava is referring.

'there is no guilt that I have not yet moved from my position, instead there is a discussion of what might give me leverage to move forwards' This reflection speaks to me of how the use of neutrality in the therapeutic process can offer a doorway from the present into future thinking. In thinking out loud about the future it is possible for clients to name or discover what will be the difference that makes a difference ....their leverage for change.

'I had the right to protection by my parents....not to be made to believe that I was bad'............I have come to understand that the naming of entitlement usually clarifies for clients what has been confusion in limbic memories sometimes so distressing as to require clients to dissociate. As we know clients frequently say they clearly remember their younger smaller self knowing something was not right about adult caretakers behaviour towards them. But as defenceless children feeling compelled to accept whatever adults in their life tell them in order to maintain some connection with those on whom they as children are totally dependent for survival. Such acceptance meant shutting down their own feelings and thoughts to such an extent that they came to believe as true, however distorted and damaging, what abusive or neglectful adults say about them. So when as a therapist I am clear with clients about what is acceptable and not acceptable adult behaviour towards children and

young people in their care, clients' sense of something not being right is validated and the mists of confusion can begin to dissolve.

'*This idea of a logical self-preservation has been a source of strength for me*' Uncovering the emotional logic of how clients' built in self-preservation mechanisms have driven behaviours now distressing and disturbing in their lives is a necessary stage in developing a coherent and liveable with story.

KATHERINE
Reframing was something you used a lot and I still find it helpful Working together with clients to create different ways of looking at a situation, person or relationship can when a truly collaborative and slowed down process be significant in providing clients not only with a different lens through which to see but also an experience of altered meaning making.

Don't you dare ask me to change I'm lost already When clients can voice their hopelessness about the possibility of change an opportunity presents itself for revisiting and reminding ourselves of the therapeutic contract. We can usefully review where we now find ourselves in our work together and amend as needed the therapeutic contract given clients' current doubts, fears and aspirations all of which make sense in the present moment.

Please fix me so my family and friends can tolerate me but don't ask me to judge them or demand changes from them. They are right....it's heretical to think otherwise and I am a bad person because I do. It is this kind of childhood legacy of needing to be loyal to the distorted and damaging beliefs of neglectful or abusing caretakers that frequently drives the wish to be able to 'cope' instead of change. Sometimes what emerges in conversation is that this complex dynamic also fuels clients' shame. Shame about who they are, as defined by significant others on whom their defenceless younger selves depended for survival. Uncovering the origins of shame in clients' lives permits the noun 'shame' to become a verb 'being shamed'. By asking when, where, how and with whom did this shaming occur the experience of feeling shame can begin to be deconstructed and seen as a relational process.

'*You didn't give up on me, held onto the hope of change for me...*' When part of clients' contract with the therapist this can both relieve clients of the burden of feeling they are supposed to be making progress and changing while simultaneously conveying both respect for where the clients find themselves at that moment without letting go of the belief that change is possible.

SARAH

'*neuroscience*' It is important to me to offer clients a framework for understanding the difference between reactivity and response-ability. So ensuring clients know about the tripartite brain and how their unwanted and distressing behaviour patterns originate in the 'old' brain and represent their fight, flight, freeze or submit reactions to perceived or real danger is crucial. I have found this reactivity can usefully be named as a 'default' position, programme or pattern and since we all have such default positions the distressing and unwanted behaviour patterns do not need to be pathologised. Instead these behaviours can be approached with curiosity and compassion because after all they originated as survival strategies.

'*I had a desire to thrive not just survive .... Couldn't really envisage what a flourishing Sarah would look like.*' Frequently I invite clients to consider the idea that we humans as part of the natural world are designed to flourish and there is a continuum of behaviour with survival at one end and flourishing at the other (Hanson 2013).

I have come to see in my work that enormous amounts of emotional energy are required by clients to hold back from naming what they don't like/want in their lives because of old taboos that frequently say 'I am not allowed to say what I want or don't want.' So risking disloyalty to an aspect of the family of origin story is a difficult and important step towards recovery of self, healing and flourishing (Boszormenyi-Nagy 1987).

My experience is that only when clients have the time and space and feel safe enough to share and name what for them is what they no longer want to be doing or feeling does space open up for them to discover what they do want. Since it is usually clear that it is their survival strategies that are the behaviours they want to give up and what they say they want to be doing instead is what they believe they need to be doing in order to flourish these discoveries absolutely need to belong to the client.

'*I had a huge need for self compassion and to forgive myself.*' Self-compassion and the wish to forgive oneself are important aspects of clients' changing relationships with themselves and their significant others, re editing family mythology and reclaiming agency of their lives. Self-compassion is closely linked to self-acceptance and self-validation as clients can then begin to allow themselves to be seen.

If you the reader are now thinking I missed important themes and/or the opportunity to comment on specific issues Ava, Katherine or Sarah highlight I can only say 'good' as this is what reflective processes are all about .... celebrating the enriching creativity of sharing different perspectives is distinctively systemic.

In conclusion here are Sarah, Katherine and Ava's responses to three questions I invite them to address:

> *Is there anything in what you are reading that resonates with where you are now in your own journey that you are willing to share?*
> *What do you notice about how you are reacting (feelings and thoughts) to what you are reading that seems relevant to share?*
> *Anything else you want to share.*

LAST WORDS FROM SARAH, KATHERINE and AVA

SARAH

Is there anything in what you are reading that resonates with where you are now in your own journey that you are willing to share?

'Today, I feel like I'm really flourishing. I have been able to let go of many of my survival strategies which had become such blocks to personal development and also barriers in my relationships with others. By letting go of these strategies I have been able to discover who I am and to find some self-acceptance. The negative messages from childhood are now just faint whispers. I have also been able to take down the walls that I built around myself and to develop authentic and close relationships with others.'

What do you notice about how you are reacting (feelings and thoughts) to what you are reading that seems relevant to share?

'As I read through this chapter, I felt sadness and compassion for the lost child that I once was. But through therapy I have found self-compassion and acceptance for who I am now and the journey has been truly transformative'.

KATHERINE

'What's interesting is how much of what Ava and Sarah have written resonates for me too, even though they were dealing with different issues. In particular, that sense of a little flame, a tiny part of me kept safe in spite of what I was going through that you helped me to identify and acknowledge.

What I have written is obviously a distillation of a long, drawn out process and is what seems most relevant to me at this moment in time. But I know that as time goes by other elements of our discussions will resurface as life continues to challenge me to honour myself. What strikes me in your observations is your clarity about what was going on for me and your willingness and patience to walk alongside me while I worked this out for myself without judgement and with compassion and understanding.'

AVA

'To read back my words gives me that rollercoaster feeling of fear—breaking the last taboo of allowing myself to be seen and heard—albeit anonymously. It is hard to let go of those untrue 'truths' of childhood but to have voiced them here shows me how far I have journeyed with you.

It has brought back a memory, how when I used to try to talk about the past a shutter would come down in my mind, leaving me mute. Screaming inside to speak but afraid to utter a word. With you I have learnt to speak the unspeakable. I notice right now I am experiencing some of this fear, that I have broken my silence. But it is my story, my past, my truth. I am not yet entirely comfortable with it—but 'it takes as long as it takes'.

———

we compose our lives from both pleasant and unpleasant materials, but the painful materials are harder to talk about. (Mary Catherine Bateson)

References

ACE: Adverse Childhood Experience Studies. (1998). *American Journal of Preventative Medicine, 14*(4), 245–258.

Andersen, T. (1987). The reflecting team: Dialogues and dialogues about dialogues. *Family Process, 26,* 415–428.

Bateson, G. (1972). *Steps to an ecology of mind.* San Francisco: Chandler Publishing Company.

Bateson, M. C. (1990). *Composing a life.* New York: Plume Books and Penguin Books.

Boszomenyi-Nagy, I. (1987). *Foundations of contextual therapy: Collected papers.* New York: Brunner Mazel.

Bowlby, J. (1988). *A secure base.* London: Psychology Press.

Byng Hall, J. (1979). Re-editing family mythology during family therapy. *Journal of Family Therapy, 1*(2), 103–116.

Cecchin, G., Lane, G., & Ray, W. A. (1994). *The cybernetics of prejudices in the practice of psychotherapy.* London: Karnac Books.

Crittenden, P. (2000). *The organisation of attachment relationships, maturation, culture and context.* New York: Cambridge University Press.

Ecker, B., Ticic, R., & Hulley, L. (2012). *Unlocking the emotional brain.* London and New York: Routledge.

Gilbert, P. (2009). Introducing compassion focussed therapy. *BJPsych Advances in Psychiatric Treatment, 15*(3), 199–208.

Hanson, R. (2013). *Hardwiring happiness.* London and New York: Ebury Publishing.

Maturana, H., & Varela, F. (1980). *Autopoiesis and cognition.* Dordrecht, Holland: D. Reidel Publishing.

Miller, S., Bargmann, S., Chow, D., & Seidel, J. (2016). *Feedback informed treatment (FIT): Improving the outcome of psychotherapy one person at a time.* New York: Springer.

Neff, K. (2010). Self compassion: An alternative conceptualisation of a healthy attitude toward oneself. *Self and Identity, 2*(2), 85–101.

Rogers, C. (1957). The necessary and sufficient conditions of therapeutic personality change. *Journal of Consulting Psychology, 21,* 95–203.

Schon, D. (1983). *The reflective practitioner.* London: Basic Books.

Schore, A. (2015). *Affect regulation and the origin of the self: The neurobiology of emotional development.* London and New York: Taylor & Francis.

Selvini Palazzoli, M., Boscolo, L., Cecchin, G., & Prata, J. (1978). *Paradox and counterparadox*. New York: Jason Aronson.

Tomm, K. (1988). Interventive interviewing part 3 intending to ask lineal, circular, strategic, or reflexive questions? *Family Process, 27*(1), 1–15.

Watzlawick, P., Beavin, J., & Jackson, D. (1967). *Pragmatics of human communication*. New York: W. W. Norton.

Winnicott, D. (1965). *Maturational processes and the facilitating environment: Studies in the theory of emotional development*. London: Hogarth Press.

5

Journeying Together Through a Landscape of Uncertainty: Long-Term Systemic Work with Young People

Sarah Houston

Early in my career in mental health, I was only interested in working with adults. It seemed to me adults could really engage with a therapist, more or less conversing at the same level. Unlike the stereotypical sulky teen, adults would choose to come to therapy, and therefore they would be willing participants, open to working together to resolve whatever challenges they were experiencing. Admittedly this was largely based on my extensive research of one person's engagement with therapy (me—quite subjective, really), but it made sense to me at the time. However, after three years in the adult mental health services I became disenchanted with the pervasive pessimism of the system in relation to chronic mental distress. I felt it to be contagious, passing from staff to staff, client to client, and watched with sinking heart the hope seep out of so many of the adults I encountered. Then, during the course of my work, the opportunity arose to run some groups for the children of adults attending the service, offering age-appropriate psychoeducation and support through play-based learning and activities. And there it was. Unlike

S. Houston (✉)
Children's Health Ireland (CHI) at Crumlin, Dublin, Ireland

© The Author(s) 2020
A. Vetere and J. Sheehan (eds.), *Long Term Systemic Therapy*,
Palgrave Texts in Counselling and Psychotherapy,
https://doi.org/10.1007/978-3-030-44511-9_5

everyone else I met in my role, despite appalling adversity, these boys and girls seemed to be immune to the contagion. They bounced into our crumbling health centres full of chat, cheek, passion and noise, and it was like someone opening a window. It was not hope that flooded in, but the possibility of hope.

Over time, I became aware that what made hope possible in those interactions was a capacity in children and young people not to be defined by their problems, and I was drawn to this hope. Soon after this, I applied for a job in the Child and Adolescent Mental Health Services (CAMHS), and within a year, I had started family therapy training. Initially the idea of working with young people was something I approached with trepidation. I likely had in mind something resembling "the stony face of a silent teen sitting in front of an oh-so-gently probing therapist" (Sasson Edgette 2012). It was many years before I was really able to recognise that the reticence I so dreaded was what the young people I now work with describe as nervousness, apprehension, guardedness, awkwardness and shyness. As one young person put it:

> "I think going into like a room, … meeting someone you didn't know and just, like, speaking to them as if you kind of do know them, I think it's really weird."

The focus of this chapter is on long-term work with young people and their families. It is hard to define what is meant by "long-term". Brief systemic therapies, such as solution-focused brief therapy, are often considered to be six sessions or less in duration (Gingerich and Eisengart 2000). Comparative studies might allow up to 20 sessions over a six-month period to qualify as short-term therapy, and from 18 months up to five years as long-term (Knekt et al. 2016; Jyrä et al. 2017; Fonagy et al. 2015). It should also be considered that relatively short periods of time spent in therapy can seem much longer to a child or young person than to an adult. When I reflect on the work I do with young people, rather than thinking of "long-term" as a particular duration, I tend to think of it more in terms of approach. In other words, I have a long-term *positioning* in relation to my clients. This means as far as possible working in a way that is not time-limited, but neither limited by other constraints such as content (what we can talk about), participants (who can come), materials (what we use), methods (how we talk) and so on. With this long-term positioning, the therapy should simply take as long as the young person needs.

In this chapter, I consider such long-term work with young people and their families from three key angles: their multiple contexts; the therapeutic relationship; and the therapeutic journey. In writing the chapter, I draw on my experience of working with young people and their families over the past fifteen years in CAMHS, in private practice, and in specialist sexual abuse services. Recently I have had the privilege of speaking with some of the young people I work with about their experiences of therapy. Along with their parents, they have kindly allowed me to reproduce some of their thoughts and ideas here.

Contexts

When young people come to therapy, it is rarely their idea (all the young people I spoke with felt "made to come" to therapy), and it is never on their own. While older adolescents may choose to come by themselves, they bring with them a host of invisible others. Beside the immediacy of the young people's family and peer relationships, there also exist the particular social and cultural contexts in which their lives are situated, and together these represent a cacophony of voices.

The Developmental Context

In meeting with a young person, I try to attend to their uniqueness and individuality without losing sight of the universal developmental context of adolescence. Understanding the context is important. For example, one young person notes that:

> "every adult was a teenager, and to forget kind of how you were when you were 15, if you're now 30 or 35, is kind of stupid."

However, if I try to tap into my fifteen year-old-self, I must take care to remember that I do so through the filter of experience, and not diminish the differences between the developmental stages of adolescence and adulthood. Teenagers are not just mini-adults, but neither should we fall into the trap of seeing them as big kids. Adolescence is a period of intense biological, psychological and social development (Santrock 2016), when a young person is moving out of childhood, and into adulthood. The enormity of this task has the potential to be extremely stressful, especially when there are other pressures within the family or social system which can distract from, complicate and confound this task. The young people I spoke to talked about both the complexity and simplicity of adolescence.

> "We have complex thoughts, but a lot of it is really simple and a lot of it is based on insecurity and the need for validation from other people besides your parents ... There are so many factors in a teenager's life now with the introduction of media, and new types of clothes, and new places you can visit, and globalization – all these things. But at the same time there is still the basic need to fit in, to want to fit in."

The Social Context

In my experience with young people, wanting to fit in (and sometimes its converse—wanting to be different) strikes me as one of the dominant scripts of adolescence. It is about identity, how the world sees us, how we see ourselves. When a young person enters the therapy space, their social context comes with them, and if the therapist cannot see that context, then understanding the pressures that the young person is experiencing becomes much harder. One of the early questions I ask young people is about their friends. Often, we end up drawing elaborate maps that resemble messy, arrow-strewn Venn diagrams. These become fluid representations of the young person's social context across time. Asking about the social context often opens a pathway that cuts through the guardedness, nervousness and apprehension of that first session. A genuine interest in a young person's life with their peers shows that you are interested in them, not just in what's "wrong" with them;

"[I] knew you cared and wanted to help cos you were so – like – interested in everything, like further circles of friends and things like that."

The Family Context

While the presence of parents can be reassuring to the young person in a first session, and some young people opt to have all their sessions conjoint, in the majority of cases the young person will be keen to have some space *"just for me"*. This can be helpful in establishing a connection between the therapist and young person, as well as offering an opportunity to speak about things that would be too difficult to talk about with parents there;

"I think it's better when it's just us two [siblings], because I think we say more when it's us two, because – like – our parents don't really relate to us as much … by that I mean they don't know what we're talking about some of the time, so – like – we don't really say, cos it's a bit more – like – awkward to say it."

However, in working systemically with young people, it is essential that the other voices remain present in the room, whether actually there or not. Individual space for the young person is important, but limited, and an overemphasis on it can risk the therapist "replac[ing] the primary caregiver as central to the change process" (Smith 2017, p. 63), and becoming overly aligned with one part of the family system. A parent spoke to me about this complex intertwining of therapeutic relationships in this way:

"you had been involved with [the young person], or we had been involved with you, or we were all involved with each other."

Conversely, Wilson notes that an overemphasis on the system risks "push[ing] the therapist's focus away from the child's own concerns when this may well be a useful place to begin" (2017, p. 103). Wilson suggests taking a both/and position in relation to the child and the system. Therefore, in my work who comes to which session is decided collaboratively and can depend on what is happening inside and outside the therapy.

In situations where relationships are very strained, and people cannot sit together, it is often possible for the therapist to become a "bridge" between young people and parents, offering individual sessions to both, where key thoughts can be transmitted between the family members' sessions, with the therapist as a conduit. Marsha McDonough describes using a similar approach in which "our meetings resembled a lively form of musical chairs with family members rotating in and out of my office, expressing their points of view" (McDonough and Koch 2007, p. 176). The ability to contain and hold everyone, while moving fluidly between the individual and the family is a particular skill of the systemic therapist. Even in individual work, the systemic lens invites in the voices of absent others through dialogue that is both circular and relational (Penn 1982; Tomm 1987a, 1987b, 1988; White 2007).

In consulting with young people, it seems to me that this connection with family can be the cornerstone of therapeutic change. It offers an opportunity for parents and children to hear each other in a different way, without the risk of conflict overwhelming the communication.

> *"I know, obviously, we can't solve all of our problems in here, but it's nice to at least have a few chances to talk about kind of more sensitive things, without a fear on either of our sides of being – you know – hurt."*

Neither is conjoint work necessarily about managing conflict. Parents often take on the role of unconditionally loving witnesses to the young person's pain, worry and woundedness. Equally, they may be witnessing their child's resilience and wonderfulness, and the young person experiences their radical acceptance of them. The young person also has the opportunity to witness their "distributed self" (Tomm 1998, p. 411) in this wise and kind other. One parent told me they felt that:

> *"I was able to maybe articulate or bring up some of the stuff that [the young person] might have found it harder to do."*

For this parent and young person, the process of being in therapy together helped resolve a lot of difficulty for the young person themselves, but at the same time strengthening and enriching their relationship. The young person told me:

> *"we always did have a good relationship … but I don't think it would be half as good."*

The Cultural Context

While there is wide variation and diversity across geographical, social and ethnic backgrounds, one of the widest gulfs across adolescent culture is generational. This presents a challenge to therapists who are invariably much older than their teenage clients, and whose experience of adolescent culture would therefore have been very different. When I speak with teenagers and their families about how they connect with their peers, I am often reminded of my own experience of sitting just behind the kitchen door, as far as the phone cord would stretch, making the best attempt I could at an embarrassingly private conversation, while the whole family sat just five feet away, ears cocked, pretending not to listen. The overlap in emotional content is similar, but almost everything else in the landscape has changed. Such low-tech communication is incommensurably foreign to our twenty-first-century teens.

All the young people I spoke to felt it was important that the therapist had some understanding of youth culture in order to be able to understand and relate to them. A parent of one of the young people explained that

> *"I don't think you ever do know, cos you can't immerse yourself in another time."*

Therefore, we must remain curious, and learn what we need to know from the young people we see. This is not an unfamiliar concept and is rooted in hermeneutics: "in order to be able to ask, one must want to know, and that means knowing that one doesn't know" (Gadamer 2004, p. 357). As we would relate to any family regarding their particular cultural context, we must join with each young person's unique cultural context by "bending towards" them, "realizing the other in his particular existence" (Buber 1965, pp. 22–23).

I don't need to be a teenager to connect with a teenager, but I do need to really listen to them with genuine, authentic interest and, as Wilson advocates, attempt to "see from behind the eyes of the child" (2017, p. 94). At the same time as knowing what we do not know, we can also draw on what we do know;

> *"everyone who has reached adulthood has been through adolescence, and should be able to tap into those memories."*

Allowing memories of the therapist's own adolescence to be accessed within the therapeutic process can enrich the therapeutic connection and facilitate greater understanding. This is a concept that Jensen refers to as "reciprocal resonance" (Jensen 2016). However, the therapist must also guard against an over-reliance on or investment in their own experience. This can lead to "therapeutic colonization", or even "therapeutic imperialism" where the therapist "may lose his or her curiosity and openness and let his or her own private situation govern the therapy session" (Jensen 2016, p. 44). There are times, therefore, when I might need to tune less into sameness and more into difference. At these times, I tend to invite more of the young person's individuality into the space, with questions chosen to elicit the differences between us.

This intricate weaving of our experiences and knowledges is central to the therapeutic journey and takes time to be established. This sets such a way of working apart from shorter term approaches which tend to be more outcome-oriented. With such methods there is less room for context, other than that which is relevant to the focus of the work. Briefer work of necessity means that the therapist loses the luxury of attending to all of the threads of the young person's life, and the richness of these multiple contexts can be lost in the drive towards a predefined goal. At the same time, it is worth noting that this kind of therapy-without-limits, which I have described as a long-term positioning, is something of a luxury both for clients and therapists. I am privileged to work in a public sector service where therapy is largely offered for as long as it is needed by the young people and families who attend. However, in all public systems resources are limited and, more often than not, impose limits on the duration of therapy or on the criteria for access. Within the private system, personal resources impact access to therapy. One young person noted:

> *"If we were from a different post code, or if [my parents] had different jobs, or if they didn't even have jobs I wouldn't be able to do this."*

Relationship

As we know from extensive research in the area of common factors, the therapeutic relationship is one of the most significant variables in predicting outcomes in psychotherapy (Norcross and Lambert 2005), perhaps especially so in working with young people (Lavik et al. 2018). For therapists, the idea of engaging young people can be daunting, and the first session in particular. It can be helpful to remember that there is so much more at risk for the young person than the therapist. The therapist has chosen to be there, the young person in all likelihood has not. The therapist usually has a referral, and quite possibly has had conversations with parents and other professionals. The young person generally has no idea what to expect. One young person explained their anxiety about the first session in this way:

> *"So, if you were really religious, which was what I was afraid of the first time, I was like 'God, she's going to talk about God, she's going to make angels pray for me, and I'm going to hate this' ... that would be the worst thing."*

The therapist must take care not to compensate for awkwardness with an over-focus on assessment, outcomes, goals and so on, as they risk losing the opportunity to genuinely meet and connect with the young person. My primary hope for the first session is to pave the way for a second session. According to the young people I spoke with, there are critical key elements for the therapist in engaging in therapy with young people. These could broadly be divided into three areas; connection, positioning and skills. While these ideas are drawn from my informal conversations with a small number of young people, it is interesting to note a significant correlation with more formal research studies such as Lavik et al. (2018), in terms of what young people want from their psychotherapist.

Connection

The young people spoke about the need for a connection with the therapist, to feel a sense of "*camaraderie*". This is in the first instance about finding a "*common ground*" and being "*comfortable*" with one another. They all used the word "*relationship*" to try and explain the connection, and some named "*dialogue*" as central to this. In long-term therapy there is no schedule to be followed. While the uncertainty of such a stance may pose challenges to the therapist (and to the young person), it also offers the opportunity to really slow down the process of connecting. Shorter term, and in particular manualised, approaches often necessitate a pace that neglects the nuance of relationship formation, with a focus on strategy rather than connection (see for example Lock and LeGrange 2012).

In speaking of both real and imagined negative experiences of therapeutic relationship, the young people said things like:

> "*they don't really get to know like what it's like for you – em – cos they're just – like – moving on with the next question.*"

A genuine dialogical meeting demands that therapists bring themselves into the space. Smith refers to Frosch's question "Does anyone still believe that it is possible for a therapist to offer something personal in therapy, to use his or her own imaginative capacity to lend a thinking presence to the other?" (Frosch 1997, p. 93). Smith contends that this is in fact "necessary if therapy is not just talking or telling stories but something truly transforming and healing" (Smith 2017, p. 64).

The young people I spoke with identified not knowing the therapist, and not knowing what to expect as potential barriers to engagement. Sometimes when I can see the young person is very ambivalent or anxious about engaging in therapy, I spend a lot of the first session just letting them know things about me. Roberts (2005) notes that research tends to support therapist self-disclosure as helpful to clients (Hill et al. 1988; Knox et al. 1997; Hanson 2004), and this is supported by Lavik et al.'s research with young people (2018). In my own experience, the bringing of one's self into the room in this tangible way can ease the awkwardness and "weirdness" of the initial and subsequent meetings, can address and positively impact the power dynamic, and can open a pathway to trust. According to the young people, trust is fundamental to the relationship and to the potential for therapeutic change. We cannot expect trust to be fully formed in those initial meetings, but from the outset that first meeting is where the seeds of trust will be sown or discarded. Again, the process of building trust does not benefit from time-limits. Trust is foundational, and without it the complex structure of therapeutic change is fundamentally compromised: "*it takes a while to build a relationship*". One young person thought they had taken about six months to "*settle in*" to therapy, but when that finally happened, said they felt that:

> "*once you build up a relationship with somebody, and once you have trust, I think you don't have a worry.*"

Despite what may be accepted psychotherapeutic convention, any therapist who adopts the position that Sasson Edgette refers to as "therapeutic bromide, 'We're not here to talk about me. We're here to talk about you'" (2012) has already dismissed an opportunity to connect. A therapeutic relationship is what Anderson describes as a "dynamic dialogical process: a two-way process that involves a back-and-forth, give-and-take, in-there-together connection and activity in which people talk with, not to, each other" (Anderson 2007, p. 47).

Positioning

The potential for genuine dialogue in therapy is often rooted in the therapist's orientation. Anderson speaks of her approach to therapy as a "philosophical stance" or a "'way of being' in relationship and conversation" (Anderson 1997, 2007, 2012; Holmes 1994). Similarly, Rober emphasises the primacy of the therapist's relational responses within a dialogue between living persons (Rober 2017). In this way, we understand there can be no how-to guide for therapists working with young people, as it is much less what the therapist *does* than how the therapist *is* that matters. The young people themselves articulate this by speaking of the need for the therapist to be open, respectful, interested in them and not to judge them. In their descriptions I am reminded of Anderson's way of being in therapy;

> I have found it helpful to think of it as if the client begins to hand me a 'story ball.' As they put the ball toward me, and while their hands are still on it, I gently place my hands on it but I do not take it from them. I begin to participate with them in the storytelling, as I slowly look at/listen to the aspect that they are showing me. I try to learn about and understand their story by responding to them: I am curious, I pose questions, I make comments, and I gesture. (Anderson 2007, p. 47)

Another significant theme for the young people I spoke with was that of care. More than liking them, or being like them, young people want to know their therapist cares about them and about what happens to them. One parent spoke of feeling that a service "*didn't take good care*" of their child, and how devastating this was. Another young person said:

> "*we want attention and validation and fitting in … and if someone's coming to you then they need that from you.*"

While the therapist can use their skills to convey care, they cannot fake it. Genuine care is necessary to convey care, and for me this means finding something I love in each person in the room. According to Rober (after Shotter 2016) "to love someone is … to notice and be responsive to the possibilities for further development in his/her being – to be the voice inviting him/her to develop into what he/she can become; as he/she is that voice for you" (Rober 2017, p. 3). As I enter into this compassionate and loving space, I am drawing on more than my stories and narratives of adolescence. Inevitably I am pulling at threads of my emotional being and experience; summoning up rich memories of being loved, attended to, validated, forsaken, betrayed and rejected. This is a risky business. Being open in this way risks my own exposure and vulnerability, but I take these risks on behalf of the vulnerable young people who come to therapy stripped of all their defences, in pain, and so much less powerful than I am. In her research on family therapists' experience of working with young people who self-harm, Richardson notes that some therapists "expressed the view that if you don't take relational risks, conversely '*you don't create a place of safety*'. The process of building trust and safety laid the foundation for taking therapeutic risks" (Richardson 2017, p. 14). This leads me to wonder how it might feel for the young people and their families to see in my wet eyes that their pain has touched off the edges of my own, that we can sit for a time in that dark place, and tolerate it together, and not be destroyed by it.

Skills

In working with young people, I tend to think about skills in terms of navigation. It is how we support and guide them in their therapy journey that defines this skill set. So, for example, the pace of the process is important. Even within the minute interactions of the therapeutic encounter, rhythm and tempo are critical, so the young person experiences the therapist as patient, not rushing.

> *"I liked the fact that there was no rush or like it was always kind of there if I needed it."*

The therapist must stick with the young person in the dialogue, not allow them to feel dismissed. In short-term work, the pace is often dictated by the pre-agreed length of treatment, as therapists and clients seek to meet certain goals or complete stages within the allotted timeframe. While such interventions have often been judged to be efficient and effective in reducing symptoms and other presenting difficulties (e.g. Srinivasan et al. 2019), it is not possible for the therapist and young person or family genuinely to collaborate on pace, and so the process is at risk of becoming an expert-led delivery of intervention as opposed to a dialogical process.

Skills in listening and responding are also critical. From a therapist perspective, this is languaged and understood through eloquent metaphors like Anderson's story ball, but for my young clients it is much simpler:

> *"you kind of understand things without us having to explain them that much ... like – relate to what we're talking about even if you don't know the topic or something ... like – if we're just – like – describing something a little bit you kind of like figured out what we're talking about if we don't really want to say it."*

I understand this young person's comments as meaning that I am listening really hard and responding in a way that means they *feel* heard. Under the surface this type of skilled listening takes a lot of work. Shotter and Katz have used the term "responsive reflective talk" (Shotter and Katz 2007, p. 19) to refer to a type of listening where intimacy and familiarity are forged to the extent that those involved "feel 'recognized' as who they are" (Shotter and Katz 2007, p. 20). This involves the therapist occupying multiple positions. I am in dialogue with my own inner talk, which Penn describes as "a balance I try to strike between emotionally following clients and assessing my feelings – what is happening to me – and listening to my own questions at the same time" (Penn 2007, p. 101). Rober depicts this as an inner dialogue between "the experiencing self" and "the professional self" (Rober 2005, p. 487). The outer talk invokes in the therapist emotions, memories, observations and intentions, which become part of this dialogue, and eventually lead to an outer response (ibid.). At another level, while sitting in my own seat, I am simultaneously attempting to occupy the other's seat, and as such I am engaging at some level with the inner talk of the other, as I consider how they might be connecting with their own inner voice. How is this landing with them? What might this be evoking in them? When there is more than one other in the room, this process is magnified exponentially, and becomes an unravelling tapestry of voices.

The therapist must also skilfully navigate the sharing of information, particularly between the young person and parents. It is essential to be clear from the start where the boundaries are drawn. As therapist I am not a figure of authority like a parent or teacher, but neither am I a best friend. The young person needs to feel confident that I will not go running to the parent with things that they are trying to work out for themselves, potentially risking the parents *"getting mad"*. But they also need to trust that I will do what is necessary to keep them safe. At the same time, I have a parallel responsibility to the parents who are also part of the therapeutic system. They are allowing me the privilege of spending one-to-one time with their young person, and need to be assured that I will not withhold from them if their child is at risk of significant harm. Within this system of boundaries there is a third level—a perimeter fence, perhaps—which is what I am required to share outside of the family system. An increasing awareness around issues of child protection has led in many jurisdictions to mandatory guidelines for reporting risk to children. Clarity of boundaries from the start gives everyone the option of making informed choices about how much to share, and how and when to share it. The ability to move around within the system, containing and holding each person's right to privacy, without keeping "secrets", and with one eye always on the possibilities for bringing forth the "not-yet-said" (Anderson 1997, p. 118), demands from the therapist significant skill.

Dowling and Vetere (2017) have asked if we have become too dependent on words and questions in our work with families. Working with young people requires the therapist to develop their skills in a more creative and playful practice;

"I just really liked the session where you were – like – 'who – like – feels the most – like – frustrated, and – like – stressed', and we – like – sat in the chairs – I liked that … I think that really worked – we didn't really have to say anything."

This young person was referring to a whole family session which had occurred early on in the therapy. I remember the young adolescents would speak little in the sessions, and almost inaudibly. I wondered if the pressure on the family from the weight of their worries was strangling their potential to communicate with each other and with me. I suggested we play a game, where the family would arrange themselves in a line in the room from "most" to "least" according to a series of descriptors which I would call out ("happy!", "worried!", "frustrated!", "likely to hide feelings!"). The catch was that they were not allowed to speak to each other in the process. This was a somewhat impulsive move on my part, in that I had not planned it, and had never played this "game" before. In my family therapy training, I benefitted from the input of therapists like Jim Wilson, Janine Roberts and Peter Rober who provided a solid grounding in the use of spontaneous play (Wilson 1998, 2007; Roberts 1994; Rober 1998, 2008). This taught me to draw on whatever fits each unique therapeutic situation from my repository of playful, personal and professional experiences and learning.

As a systemic therapist, language is my core medium, and it is easy to forget how hard it can be for young people to articulate their feelings, especially with parents present. Games, art and drama all afford an opportunity to communicate without words and bring the added benefit of lightening the seriousness of the issues that can saturate a family (White and Epston 1990; Freeman et al. 1997). When a family feels this bound by problems, the physical act of moving can initiate a first-order change. And this first-order loosening of the system then has the potential to lead to a second-order shift. In adopting creative strategies, we find ourselves borrowing from our colleagues in the areas of play therapy, art therapy, drama therapy and others, and this can come under criticism or resistance from the systemic community (Wilson 2017). However, the skill here is always to remain systemic in our use of these approaches and techniques. Such approaches enhance systemic therapy, they do not replace it. A secure grounding in systemic practice is essential to the safe and beneficial implementation of such techniques, so as Flaskas puts it "rather like riffing in jazz, the conditions of therapeutic creativity and improvisation emerge alongside a discipline and focus in learning" (Flaskas 2013, p. 289).

Journey

Early on in the therapy I often ask the question "how would you know if you didn't need to come to therapy anymore?" The answers I get, typically hesitant and tentative, are invariably connected to the idea of change, although *what* should change is not always clear, consistent across time nor the same for each person in the room. Regrettably, in systemic psychotherapy research, change is often defined by the researcher. Studies that focus on outcomes or "what works" in therapy for adolescents consider what is measurable, and this tends to be quite narrow, often focusing on the presence or absence of "symptoms" (Cottrell and Boston 2002; Carr 2019). This was not something that the young people I spoke with referenced, however, a common theme among them was "resolving". There was a sense of therapy being "*a good place to straighten things out*". For the young people this seems to be connected to relational change, change in how the young person feels, and change in what can be talked about.

In order for the therapist to really connect with the young person and their system, and to hear what matters to them, they need to be able to resist the draw towards time-limited, symptom-based and outcome-driven practices. In this way, I find attending to the journey more helpful than the goal. When I am invited to speak to family therapy trainees about my practice, I often refer to the metaphor of tangled jewellery. The family bring their precious knotted jewels to my room, and together we sit and gently begin to massage the knots, lightly tugging at the ends of threads as they become looser, until over the weeks and months the beautiful pieces begin to emerge. This is a slow process that requires everyone's patience, and the therapist cannot dictate the length of the journey.

> "*I think the more important things, the longer you spend, the more will come up naturally, and will just like, come to light and that's important ... it wouldn't have been that helpful for me to just unload everything in six weeks, have it all trawled through and then right, no closure, nothing, we're just going to like go back to the real world and I'll be left with kind of like the sense of well, what now? I've just unloaded everything in front of a complete stranger. What's going to happen – what am I supposed to get out of this? ...*

I think however long it takes to be able to just let things come to light is long enough whether it takes 6 weeks or 6 months or 6 years."

I add nothing to this "jewellery" but my skilled hands and my hope. I do not know what it will look like in the .end but I trust that we will know when we are there. This trust comes from my experience of walking paths like these with so many young people before. I sometimes feel like a Sherpa. These skilled navigators know the terrain. They plan the route and equip themselves and the climbers for the journey. They prepare themselves for the unexpected. They provide the climber with sustenance and take the weight of their bags. In this vision of the process, I am drawn to Weingarten's ideas on hope, and in particular to her concept of "accompaniment" (Weingarten 2004, 2010). Weingarten describes the therapist's task as doing *with* rather than doing *to*, so the therapist accompanies the client(s) on their journey. For young people traversing the uncertain landscape of adolescence, the most important thing may be to have someone walk alongside them, bearing witness to their pain (ibid.), and to have this happen for as long as they need. In this witnessing, the therapist must feel the client's pain, but not become overwhelmed, either by the pain, or by the risks that may be associated with it. Weingarten urges us to be "aware and empowered" witnesses (Weingarten 2010, p. 11) and that in doing so we can help clients to do the same.

When my clients speak of this journey through therapy, they speak positively and warmly of the experience. They feel it is something everyone should do (acknowledging that not everyone can afford to) and that no-one should be ashamed of. They value a trusting, supportive relationship with the therapist where the therapy is regular, frequent and long enough for a relationship to grow, and

"till – like – everything's kind of resolved … or it's got better … and you can – like – stop."

References

Anderson, H. (1997). *Conversation, language and possibilities: A postmodern approach to therapy*. New York: Basic Books.

Anderson, H. (2007). The heart and spirit of collaborative therapy: The philosophical stance—"A way of being" in relationship and conversation. In H. Anderson & D. Gehart (Eds.), *Collaborative therapy: Relationships and conversations that make a difference* (pp. 43–59). London: Routledge.

Anderson, H. (2012). Collaborative relationships and dialogic conversations: Ideas for a relationally responsive practice. *Family Process, 51*(1), 8–24.

Buber, M. (1965). *Between man and man*. New York: Macmillan.

Carr, A. (2019). Family therapy and systemic interventions for child-focused problems: The current evidence base. *Journal of Family Therapy, 41*, 153–213.

Cottrell, D., & Boston, P. (2002). Practitioner review: The effectiveness of systemic family therapy for children and adolescents. *Journal of Child Psychology and Psychiatry, 43*(5), 573–586.

Dowling, E., & Vetere, A. (2017). Narrative concepts and challenges. In A. Vetere & E. Dowling (Eds.), *Narrative therapies with children and their families: A practitioner's guide to concepts and approaches* (2nd ed., pp. 3–23). London: Routledge.

Flaskas, C. (2013). Teaching and learning theory for family therapy practice: On the art and craft of balancing. *Australian & New Zealand Journal of Family Therapy, 34*(4), 283–293.

Fonagy, P., Rost, F., Carlyle, J. A., McPherson, S., Thomas, R., Pasco Fearon R. M., et al. (2015). Pragmatic randomized controlled trial of long-term psychoanalytic psychotherapy for treatment-resistant depression: The Tavistock Adult Depression Study (TADS). *World Psychiatry, 14*, 312–321.

Freeman, J., Epston, D., & Lobovits, D. (1997). *Playful approaches to serious problems: Narrative therapy with children and their families*. New York: W. W. Norton.

Frosch, S. (1997). Postmodern narratives: Or muddles in the mind. In R. K. Papadopoulos & J. Byng-Hall (Eds.), *Multiple voices: Narratives in systemic psychotherapy* (pp. 86–102). London: Duckworth.

Gadamer, H. G. (2004). *Truth and method* (2nd ed., revised, J. Weinsheimer & D. G. Marshall, Trans.). London: Continuum.

Gingerich, W. J., & Eisengart, S. (2000). Solution-focused brief therapy: A review of the outcome research. *Family Process, 39*(4), 477–498.

Hanson, J. E. (2004). *Clients' perceptions of therapist self-disclosure as a therapeutic technique* (Unpublished thesis). Ontario Institute for Studies in Education, University of Toronto.

Hill, C. E., Helms, J. E., Tichenor, V., Spiegel, S. B., O'Grady, K. E., & Perry, E. S. (1988). Effects of therapist response modes in brief psychotherapy. *Journal of Counselling Psychology, 35,* 222–233.

Holmes, S. (1994). A philosophic stance, ethics and therapy: An interview with Harlene Anderson. *Australian and New Zealand Journal of Family Therapy, 15*(3), 155–161.

Jensen, P. (2016). Mind the map: Circular processes between the therapist, the client and the therapist's personal life. In A. Vetere & P. Stratton (Eds.), *Interacting selves: Systemic solutions for personal and professional development in counselling and psychotherapy* (pp. 33–49). London: Routledge.

Jyrä, K., Knekt, P., & Lindfors, O. (2017). The impact of psychotherapy treatments of different length and type on health behaviour during a five-year follow-up. *Psychotherapy Research, 27*(4), 397–409.

Knekt, P., Virtala, E., Härkänen, T., Vaarama, M., Lehtonen, J., & Lindfors, O. (2016). The outcome of short- and long-term psychotherapy 10 years after start of treatment. *Psychological Medicine, 46*(6), 1175–1188.

Knox, S., Hess, S. A., Petersen, D. A., & Hill, C. E. (1997). A qualitative analysis of client perceptions of the effects of helpful therapist self-disclosure in long-term therapy. *Journal of Counselling Psychology, 44,* 274–283.

Lavik, K. O., Veseth, M., Frøysa, H., Binder, P., & Moltu, C. (2018). 'Nobody else can lead your life': What adolescents need from psychotherapists in change processes. *Counselling and Psychotherapy Research, 18*(3), 262–273.

Lock, J., & LeGrange, D. (2012). *Treatment manual for anorexia nervosa: A family-based approach* (2nd ed.). New York: Guilford.

McDonough, M., & Koch, P. (2007). Collaborating with parents and children in private practice: Shifting and overlapping conversations. In H. Anderson & D. Gehart (Eds.), *Collaborative therapy: Relationships and conversations that make a difference* (pp. 167–181). London: Routledge.

Norcross, J. C., & Lambert, M. J. (2005). What should be validated? The therapy relationship. In J. C. Norcross, L. E. Beutler, & R. F. Levant (Eds.), *Evidence-based practices in mental health: Debate and dialogue on the fundamental questions* (pp. 208–218). Washington, DC: American Psychological Society.

Penn, P. (1982). Circular questioning. *Family Process, 21,* 267–280.

Penn, P. (2007). Listening voices. In H. Anderson & D. Gehart (Eds.), *Collaborative therapy: Relationships and conversations that make a difference* (pp. 99–107). London: Routledge.

Richardson, C. (2017). Cultivating the practice of hope, withstanding the pull to hopelessness: A grounded theory study of family therapists' experience of working with adolescents who self-harm. *Feedback: Journal of the Family Therapy Association of Ireland, 1,* 2–30.

Rober, P. (1998). Reflections on ways to create a safe therapeutic culture for children in family therapy. *Family Process, 37,* 201–213.

Rober, P. (2005). The therapist's self in dialogical family therapy: Some ideas about not knowing and the therapist's inner conversation. *Family Process, 44,* 477–495.

Rober, P. (2008). Being there, experiencing and creating space for dialogue: About working with children in family therapy. *Journal of Family Therapy, 30*(4), 465–477.

Rober, P. (2017). *In therapy together: Family therapy as a dialogue.* London: Palgrave Macmillan.

Roberts, J. (1994). *Tales and transformations.* New York: W. W. Norton.

Roberts, J. (2005). Transparency and self-disclosure. *Family Process, 44*(1), 45–63.

Santrock, J. W. (2016). *Adolescence* (16th ed.). New York: McGraw-Hill.

Sasson Edgette, J. (2012, September). Why teens hate therapy. *Psychotherapy Networker, 36.* Retrieved from https://ucd.idm.oclc.org/login?url=https://search-proquest-com.ucd.idm.oclc.org/docview/1151970057?accountid=14507.

Shotter, J., & Katz, A. (2007). "Reflecting talk", "inner talk", and "outer talk": Tom Andersen's way of being. In H. Anderson & P. Jensen (Eds.), *Innovations in the reflecting process: The inspirations of Tom Andersen* (pp. 16–32). London: Karnac.

Smith, G. (2017). Children's narratives of traumatic experiences. In A. Vetere & E. Dowling (Eds.), *Narrative therapies with children and their families: A practitioner's guide to concepts and approaches* (2nd ed., pp. 61–74). London: Routledge.

Srinivasan, R., Walker, S., & Wakefield, J. (2019). Cognitive behavioural therapy, short-term psychoanalytical psychotherapy and brief psychosocial intervention are all effective in the treatment of depression in adolescents. *Archives of Disease in Childhood - Education and Practice, 104,* 56.

Tomm, K. (1987a). Interventive interviewing: Part I. Strategizing as a fourth guideline for the therapist. *Family Process, 26,* 3–13.

Tomm, K. (1987b). Interventive interviewing: Part II. Reflexive questioning as a means to enable self-healing. *Family Process, 26,* 167–183.

Tomm, K. (1988). Interventive interviewing: Part III. Intending to ask lineal, circular, strategic, or reflexive questions. *Family Process, 27,* 1–15.

Tomm, K. (1998). A question of perspective. *Journal of Marital & Family Therapy, 24,* 409–413.

Weingarten, K. (2004). Commentary on Candib: What is at the centre, and what at the edges, of care? *Family, Systems and Health, 22,* 151–157.

Weingarten, K. (2010). Reasonable hope: Construct, clinical applications, and supports. *Family Process, 49*(1), 5–25.

White, M. (2007). *Maps of narrative practice.* London: W. W. Norton.

White, M., & Epston, D. (1990). *Narrative means to therapeutic ends.* New York: W. W. Norton.

Wilson, J. (1998). *Child-focused practice: A collaborative-systemic approach.* London: Karnac.

Wilson, J. (2007). *The performance of practice.* London: Karnac.

Wilson, J. (2017). Engaging children and young people: A theatre of possibilities. In A. Vetere & E. Dowling (Eds.), *Narrative therapies with children and their families: A practitioner's guide to concepts and approaches* (2nd ed., pp. 91–111). London: Routledge.

Part III

Long Term Systemic Work with Professional Practitioner Groups

6

Psychological and Emotional Support in the Workplace: Can It Make a Difference for the Longer Term?

Helga Hanks

Introduction

All through my career I have been supervising and supporting people in the workplace. In the 1970s and 1980s, while working in the old Victorian mental health Asylums, I became aware of the stress responses described by some colleagues (Don Bannister 1976, personal communication) that were not only obvious in the patients but also in the staff—from porters, to nurses, to psychiatrists, psychologists and social workers, but also for the secretaries in those institutions who typed the letters describing the conditions of individual patients. And then of course, there were the gardeners who cared not only for the plants and gardens but also for the patients who became involved in the gardening. All of the above working people could become distressed by what they saw, heard and experienced with and for the patients as well as being under stress themselves from overworking. By realising that work can be stressful in

H. Hanks (✉)
Leeds, UK

© The Author(s) 2020
A. Vetere and J. Sheehan (eds.), *Long Term Systemic Therapy*,
Palgrave Texts in Counselling and Psychotherapy,
https://doi.org/10.1007/978-3-030-44511-9_6

so many ways and at any time—and sometimes over long periods—and can lead to poor health for those working in psychologically unhealthy environments (both physically and emotionally), I understood that the workforce needed to be supported emotionally. At that time, much more than now in 2019, acknowledging and speaking about stress, distress, let alone depression or work-related burnout, would have been and was a very hard step to take. It would have been labelled as being weak and not fit for the challenges of work.

Of course the 1st and 2nd World Wars in Europe and across the world, made it possible to begin to think that being involved in the most atrocious situations in war had consequences for the soldiers and could affect their psychological health in fundamental ways. Pat Barker's fiction writing (1966) describes some of the work that was undertaken to help 'shell shocked' soldiers (Bion 1997) which is now much more understood in terms of trauma and Post Traumatic Stress Disorder (PTSD). Later research undertaken by Figley (1995), Figley and Nash (2007) gave an insight into how the understanding of the kind of stress experienced in combat situations could be transferred into areas of other professional stress. Slowly, over the years, it has become possible to recognise that stress at work can have the same consequences and thus needs our detailed attention.

Throughout the years of working as a clinical psychologist in the UK National Health Service (NHS), I have divided my work between adults, families and children in the area of child abuse. In 2001, my colleagues in Paediatrics and myself set up an innovative service to support staff, particularly Paediatricians, in their work in the area of child abuse.

I had begun to think about supporting those working in the field of Paediatrics where doctors and other staff were seeing children and their families where child abuse had occurred. I knew that all those working in this area, including myself, had been affected in many ways. Burnout was a real threat. However, at that time little was written about the matter. The most severe outcomes, like 'burnout' had been written about by Freudenberg (1974) and later Masson (1990) but back then and in many fields of work today, 'risk', as in risk to the Organisation, was and still is the main topic of concern in most Organisations. Boland (2006) wrote an important account of what can happen to professionals working in the area of child abuse, particularly if the Organisations they work in are as disorganised as some of the families. Caring for the workforce is only now becoming something that people recognise and acknowledge with relevant action. The recent BMA report (2018) that discusses how to 'care for the mental health of the medical workforce' is one such example. What we did know more about was 'trauma' and how that impacted on the person even from a very young age (Crittenden 2008). The attachment literature, research and practice at the time recognised the neurological impact of stress on infants and children, but here, I want to return to the work with staff in the UK NHS.

There is no doubt in my mind that it is difficult to build a culture in which it is acceptable for doctors, or any other professions, at whatever level in their career, to seek and/or accept emotional/psychological support. My curiosity about what medical staff and others feel, or are taught, about what it means to them when they seek support, has been heightened during the time I have worked in this field. My thinking has revolved around how to help staff not to feel somehow that they are weak or inadequate because of seeking support.

Today, in 2019, we have available a considerable literature concerned with stress in the workplace, such as Bennett et al. (2005), Maslach and Leiter (2008), Figley (2008), Hanks and Vetere (2016), BMA project (2018) and Gorvett (2019). How it affects and impacts people, what they might do about it, where it occurs, such as in financial services, government, the NHS, Universities and Education, the Police Services, and in large global companies as well as in the more local and smaller businesses is now much better understood than in the NHS, even though by definition the NHS is well aware of ill health. Stress is a major factor in NHS employees and staff not being as well as they should be is sadly a common experience (Obholzer and Roberts 1994; Lyth 1988). In April 2019, the Health Secretary for the UK, Matt Hancock, pointed out (article in *The Guardian*, 25 April 2019, page 13 by Jessica Elgot) that the NHS needed to adopt 'a more compassionate culture towards staff' and said 'that staff, amongst other issues, had to work inflexible shift and rota systems despite ill health, family tragedy or events, etc. and all because the management was unwilling to design staff rotas at a rate which encompassed the fact that it was human beings, with all their complexities, that they were dealing with'. In some way this seems such a small issue but it makes visible the intransigence that can develop in large Organisations. Losing touch with compassion and nurturing and instead creating a system of blaming, controlling and even bullying and harassment is detrimental to the individuals and ultimately to the Organisation as a whole (Reeves 2019).

Another reason why the workforce can be put under severe stress is that there are constant changes in the Organisation, such as changes in regulations and guidelines which are frequently re-edited and re-worked. In turn it can be observed that the workforce mirrors the unpredictable and often unresponsive senior layer of management as well as re-creating a blaming culture. Groups within the workforce (in the environments that I describe here) and departments can become dysfunctional and act either individually and/or collectively in many ways like the abusive families the staff work with. In my experience, this is a very important point to recognise and take action around. It is also well worth remembering here that child abuse work is unpopular, as it includes some serious and unavoidable risks for the workforce. There are numerous examples of 'medical, social work and other professional victims', and often the guidance and procedure of clinical practice is unclear. Attacks on this work and those involved in protecting children are a world-wide phenomenon.

How It Started in Leeds

With the support of some broadminded colleagues in the medical profession, who had the foresight to see that the stress of child abuse was playing havoc with staff wellbeing, we began to think about a service that might support doctors and staff when they worked in the area of child abuse. (*I would like to point out here that I use the term 'child abuse' deliberately because the currently preferred language to my mind hides the atrocious behaviour of some people towards some children when child abuse occurs. The more recent terms like 'child protection' and 'safeguarding' do not remind us of the enormity of the abuse experienced by children, rather they hide its enormity.*)

As I write the above, it is worth remembering that even in the medical professions the idea of needing psychological support to do their work was not looked upon kindly, but more as a failure in the person/staff to be strong. After all, these were the people who were supposed to be the strong ones! Also the idea of psychological support (even in the broadest sense) was thought to be what doctors offered in order to help others i.e. the patients, but not the clinicians.

So in 2002 we started the psychological support service in earnest and offered staff an opportunity to talk individually or sometimes in groups. I developed a leaflet to describe the service. The funding was for 1 session (3.5 hours) per week and I was employed by the NHS Trust. The time allocated was not much and I have to acknowledge that I often gave more time as the years passed and people became more trusting of me and the service.

Staff could make appointments to talk or I made sure if there was space to let staff know that they could come. The appointments lasted for approximately 1 hour. I also gave presentations about stress and related topics to the department. I made very clear when I was in the department and available.

What Is Psychological Support?

We used the word 'support' deliberately because we did not want to give the impression that this service provided therapy. A leaflet spelt this out and stated that: 'The support centres around any topic of work related to child protection and how this is impacting on the individual emotionally, causing anxiety, stress and uncertainty. Both work and private issues can be discussed'.

The aim of providing a service to this group of professional people was to make available psychological and emotional support in order to prevent professional and emotional harm, and to enhance the service received by children and families. The support centred mainly around topics related to work (work with children, their families, with colleagues, with management, other professionals, the Courts and so on), but very importantly I also included the notion that work in general, but child abuse work in particular, impacts on our private lives. Equally private lives impact on our work. And so all of these themes were points of discussion, though entirely the choice of the professional. An integration of systemic as well as psychodynamic ways of thinking became paramount.

The approach to 'support' was based on a systemic framework (Dallos and Draper 2015) to understand how people function in professional systems and to think of acceptable ways for the professionals to consider alternatives. This is combined with a psychodynamic understanding of how people adapt to stress and how each individual reacts differently under circumstances where they witness the consequences of abuse or are experiencing aggression towards themselves. The boundaries between support counselling and therapy were clear in my mind and I was careful to pay attention to these distinctions. Though it must be said it proved to be easier to recognise this when we strayed into what might have seemed clinical supervision. While I advocated strongly that clinical supervision was essential, it had to be done separately and by the appropriate people.

It might not be difficult to imagine that it took some time for the support service to get under way. Although in principal people were much in favour that such a service should exist, making use of it and booking an appointment with me, took some time. The thought of speaking with someone about personal, and sometimes distressing issues was harder than it first appeared. Over time, with the experience of using the service, or seeing colleagues using the service, the hesitancy eased and the service and I were perceived as being helpful and even necessary.

During this time, it also became obvious that secretaries typing distressing material in letters and reports (whether to do with child abuse, complex severe illness or the incidence of a patient dying) was immensely upsetting and often led to the person who has typed the report or letter not being able to let go of the material, to be thinking about it for a long time, and to possibly not sleeping at night, and so on. We found that the almost 'passive' role of the secretary typing the events around the abuse was at times intensely painful and stressful to that person. The feeling of being helpless to make things better for the child was often unbearable in such situations. Support was welcomed and taken up.

An example: *A person discussed the death of a very young infant who had allegedly died because of abuse. The doctor was very distressed and as we talked about this tragic case it became clear that this person had a baby of the same age. The images and thoughts were so strong and the doctor tried to find a way of being able to go home and not discuss the happening but to explain to the spouse why this had been such a distressing day.*

Professionals need care too. Our heart goes out to those children who have suffered abuse. We feel the distress that others feel. When looking after children (and others in distress) we cannot escape being reminded of our own vulnerability. By reaching out to those children, we are also reaching out to ourselves and those we care about.

It was no surprise to find that the extended discussions which took place over many years were intensive and very wide ranging. These discussions ranged from case material, to working together with other professionals, to organisational demands and stresses, personal demands, different opinions between professionals and the Organisations they worked in. Also difficulties in the wider system were discussed, including what happened when staff were in Court presenting evidence, struggling to forge links with other disciplines, attending case conferences, and how to respond to media stories that were clearly false, and so on. The denial in the system, and in the world at large, that child abuse and particularly sexual abuse existed, was high. Those who believed the stories of the children and young people were often criticised for doing so. It was not until the Cleveland Report of Inquiry into Child Abuse in 1987 that Dame Butler-Sloss made an unequivocal judgement; 'that sexual abuse occurs in children of all ages, including the very young, to boys as well as girls, in all classes of society and frequently within the privacy of the family' (Hobbs et al. 1999). Personal attacks on those attempting to protect children were not uncommon. Some of this still exists in 2019.

These discussions were often intense and tense and showed how work and looking after patients over the years had often gone far beyond what one would have expected. The Organisation, management and staff in other departments were often totally unaware of what these nurses, doctors, therapists, secretaries, receptionists and so on, had to deal with on a daily basis. As a clinical psychologist myself it was clear that I could not take on the role of clinical supervisor for the paediatricians, or other associated professionals, but what I hoped to add to their practice was an understanding of the psychological issues surrounding their cases and the longer term psychological issues which impacted on the paediatricians themselves.

I did throughout my time with this work have supervision myself. The supervisor and I agreed on the confidentiality issues for this relatively small and identifiable group. Names were not mentioned and the group knew who the supervisor was. The supervisor did not know any of the people in the department and worked in a place far away.

Do Professionals Have a Duty to Look After Themselves?

By 2006 I was formulating the idea that professionals had a duty to look after themselves and I began to use this concept as a title in presentations at conferences and in teaching. In many professions the notion that looking after oneself is important had not been addressed specifically, either with theory or research. In my work with these professionals I was very careful not to make it sound as if they were to blame when they became stressed, tired and exhausted. I was strongly reminded by the practices in the NHS (no doubt elsewhere as well) that when vaccinations against influenza were introduced a culture of blaming grew. Because, if a member of staff became ill with influenza and had not been vaccinated they were blamed for having the influenza. As if somehow, vaccination was always a 100% protection.

I did not wish to imply that anyone suffering from stress and/or worse—burnout—could have prevented becoming ill. It is more that people in general could be made aware that there are ways of recognising that limits of stress have been reached and what steps can be taken prevent the worst outcomes. The practice of mindfulness as a general stress relief is a good example, however there has been recent research by Samra (2012) that workers who went on to develop burnout had actually better psychological health than the comparison group earlier in the study. Which suggested that those people who had training in the recognition of stressful events and the practice of mindfulness were more likely to suffer from burnout than those that did not have that preventative knowledge. But why so? Could it be that mindfulness practice emphasises the role and resilience of the individual in the context of greater stress awareness, rather than also emphasising the clear importance of social support and community action to combat the effects of prolonged exposure to stress at work. When the authors looked specifically at burnout in professionals in Medicine they found that 'A large systematic review showed that both organisational and individual interventions are effective at reducing burnout. However the interventions need to be tailored and not only rely on teaching people skills like Mindfulness. Other interventions needed to be put in place at the same time'.

I observed that staff did take on board that the emotional support in individual and long term group meetings was a useful adjunct to self care and that it was worth making use of these sessions. I also noticed that there was a greater awareness about the importance of looking after each other. It was not that some of this had not happened before, but the quality of the care changed in the context of long term participation in the support of individual and group sessions. Conversations with one another about such matters as overworking became more frequent and demanded a response: 'I recognised you were here after I left for home at 7:30 pm, so when did you leave? Have you had your lunch? Have you been able to catch up with your patient letters?' As these kinds of conversations became more frequent amongst the staff they contributed to a greater sense of cohesiveness and emotional safety. Now this did not mean that there were no 'ups and downs'. It seems inevitable that an environment which deals with abuse and violence, tragedy and stress at the highest level can also produce strife, distrust and blame. It is when there is someone who can recognise this state of affairs, spell it out and work with the staff on resolution and giving support that things can get better again. And this takes time, commitment and patience over the longer term. It may be useful to point out here that I was there for 18 years but so were many of the staff and it was the relationship, and trust that developed during this time that was an important factor in the work.

It is my long held opinion and experience that it is supportive when the workforce is helped to think of the consequences of their actions, to recognise when they have been overworking, when they have been harassed or bullied by others, and how this makes them feel stressed and possibly ill. All staff members need to know where to go to get consistent and predictable help. A recent anonymous survey about 'stress in the workplace' showed that 90% of the participants did not tell anyone that they felt so stressed they could not go to work. They gave different reasons for their absence at work. (www.bmj.com). They felt that a terrible stigma was associated with mental health—and that included stress.

When people have been fatigued, stressed and unable to work, they need a period of time for recovery. It is important to acknowledge this in the workplace. It often takes longer to recover than we all think. In this fast paced world it can mean longer than employers will allow before becoming impatient and implying that we are weak, lazy, and not pulling our weight, and so on. Thus, making sensible decisions is sometimes not easy under such pressure. But there will be more pressure if there is a recurrence of the stress and things can escalate possibly into denial of the situation and further ill health. These topics featured in our individual and group-based consultations. As trust grew between group members and myself it became more and more possible to openly and straight forwardly address the impact of the work, and to look for shared solutions. Thus, what did we learn to look out for—for ourselves and for each other? To become aware of long hours at work. To ask, can you say 'no' to the demands which mean you will work longer hours? Who will help you to say 'no'? To encourage everyone to take a break during the day, and to eat and drink sensibly at work and at home. My colleagues groan when I say, during the working week '….and forego the wine when you get home and are feeling stressed'. To pay attention to your family relationships and your social life. To meet with friends, to learn new skills, to take your holidays and all your annual leave, and so on.

There is of course a crucial and pivotal role for the Organisation too. How can we be helped to function energetically, positively and successfully in our work? Is it possible, especially if we do not have a caring, thoughtful, and honest system of appraisal and support operating in the workplace? In a recent editorial about burnout (Samra 2012) the author stated that: 'Medical workloads need to be reconfigured or redesigned in line with human cognitive, emotional and physical limitations with accompanying Organisation-wide training and management support. Active participation from the professional workforce will be key to achieving success in the development of healthier and safer medical workplaces'. Professionals have a duty to themselves and to others to take care that they do not become ill because of stress. This is not always avoidable, especially when the Organisation does not have a culture of looking after their workforce. A paper by Hutchinson (2019) discusses the role Organisations have and asks whether the Organisations have a duty to keep their employees safe, rather than the employee having to take those steps alone.. She points to the misrepresentation of aspects like safety and care and says; '…safety measures can become rigidly applied and have the unintended consequence of demotivating and disengaging people, as they signal a lack of trust and reduce autonomy'.

Trust and Resilience Operating at Work

The topic of trust has been an important one throughout the 18 years I have worked with the staff group. A definition of 'trust' looks so simple and straight forward. The dictionary says: 'reliance on the integrity, justice, etc. of a person, or on some quality or attribute of a thing' (ref the dictionary). Attachment theory defines trust as the perception of responsiveness and accessibility in the other. However, we live in a world of 'Fake News' and in a digital age which regards confidentiality with little respect. Many things we do on the computer belong to Google or Facebook or some other social media. But therapy, support, counselling and mentoring are, or have been, in essence confidential unless the patient/client gave consent to share what they have talked about. There are very few exceptions to this.

I experienced the initial hesitant approaches by the staff while keeping the above firmly in mind. We would talk about confidentiality, what the exceptions were, and when we had to think of passing information on to a line manager or clinical supervisor. I made it very clear that, in the first place, I would encourage the person to discuss the issue we both thought needed to be discussed elsewhere. This may have concerned an illness. I would ask the staff member to tell the line manager or supervisor to let me know that this had been done and broadly how the topic was covered. Otherwise our conversations remained confidential. I presumed staff checked out whether I was doing what I had said, and that they talked amongst themselves and checked out whether others had the experience of being able to trust me. The above is crucial in establishing a good, trustworthy relationships in therapy in general but becomes particularly important when working with individuals who are colleagues and work closely together in a department dealing with very sensitive matters on a daily basis.

Establishing a working relationship in therapy takes time and patience, particularly when it comes to working in the area of child abuse (Hanks and Stratton 2007). I have been concerned for a long time that the guidelines for short term therapy did not take into consideration how long it takes to establish a trusting therapeutic relationship. Three or 6 sessions during which complex problems have to be worked through are simply not enough in my experience, and in this particular working context. Thus we agreed that staff could make times to talk, and often book an appointment in advance. If we both felt that one or two meetings helped to get clarity about a difficulty, then this was fine. Meetings would generally last one hour. If we felt it needed more time we would agree further meetings. We had this flexibility. It was my role to continually monitor and negotiate this with management staff. It might be useful to mention Casement (1985, 2018) here who has encouraged me to continue over this 18 year period to see staff again and again with different difficulties but recognising that a thread might be linking specific feelings and behaviours and learn from these.

Over the years, we also agreed to meet in groups, sometimes with the whole department and more often in specialised, clinic-based groupings. Here we concentrated more on the clinical experiences staff had and how to resolve difficult matters, both clinical and administrative. In the group meetings we agreed not to talk about personal matters as such, but we did often explore what emotional feelings and thoughts we had relating to case material, to the group working together and the impact of outside influences. These included how people in administrative, or line management roles tried to make changes to the group. For example, how administrative staff tried to influence who worked in the specialist clinics, and what patient groups should be seen in the clinics. The issue concentrated on numbers and costs rather than on quality and appropriateness of staff and clients. These decisions might be made without including the group member's experiences and expertise on the matter. Here again trust became a core issue. On reflection, I realise as I am writing this that we often did not overtly speak of trust, but I always knew that it was an issue.

In this context it is essential to think about resilience and what it means for clients and staff working in areas like child abuse. There has been an explosion of papers and books on the subject and I will not go into details of the matter. However, there are a few things I would like to highlight. Resilience is not some thing we either have or do not have. What contributes to becoming resilient includes learning about it, thinking about it and considering and recognising the beliefs we hold and how we attribute cause and effect. The definition, coming originally from engineering, which states that resilience depends on 'springing back into shape or position after being stretched, bent or compressed; recovering strength after a trauma or stress' seems to describe the human condition equally well. What needs to be remembered is that everyone is different and does it differently. Being resilient does not mean that people do not feel distressed, upset, suffer from stress or from trauma. Painful emotions and sadness are a common feature in people who have become resilient. And yet—Resilience is ordinary—not extraordinary.

A warning when thinking about resilience is to remember that resilience to stress is not the same as resistance to stress. Resistance implies that stress can be carried, come what may, and that there is no consequence of stress, that it does not matter. Taking on ever more, working more and more hours, enduring painful relationships without respite is no solution.

Support and supervision for adults, support and advocacy for children, having human beings around who are kind, caring and understanding are the building blocks for developing resilience and to our wellbeing (Colette and Ungar 2020, in press) stress, resilience is an outcome of relationships and context, not an internal quality of the individual.

Conclusion

There is no doubt that the psychological support over a long time established in the department provided a stabilising framework which enabled staff to talk about their difficulties, stresses, workloads, private lives and thoughts as well as organisational failings. Having been able to see the same people over this long period has been important and contributed to preventing burnout.

The process I have described started at a time when there was little appreciation of the potential value of providing psychological support to staff, not because they were showing symptoms of distress but because of a recognition that their work situation put them at risk. The structure we created, and refined over the years, has proven of great value to the team I was working in. Because it was conducted over a long period it was able to connect well to the growing awareness of the damaging effects on staff of unreasonable work situations and the consequent costs to the Organisation. The progressive understanding of the causes and consequences of burnout is relevant here. Another current connection is to the increasing sophistication of concepts of resilience and relational interdependence.

I hope this description of the development of the work over nearly 20 years will encourage others to create similar provision for staff in stressful work, and that they will be able to draw on the recent advances to improve on what we have achieved so far.

References

Barker, P. (1966). *The regeneration trilogy*. London: Penguin Group.

Bennett, S., Plint, A., & Clifford, T. J. (2005). Burnout, psychological morbidity, job satisfaction, and stress. *Archives of Disease in Childhood, 90*, 1112–1116.

Bion, W. R. (1997). *War Memoirs 1917–19*. London: Karnac Books.

BMA Report. (2018). *Caring for the mental health of the medical workforce.*

Boland, C. (2006). Functional families: Functional teams. *ANZJFT, 27*(1), 22–28.

Butler-Sloss, E. (1988). *Report of the inquiry into child abuse in Cleveland 1987.* London: HMSO.

Casement, P. (1985). *Learning from the patient.* London: Routledge.

Casement, P. (2018). *Learning along the way: Further reflections on psychoanalysis and psychotherapy.* London: Routledge.

Collette, A., & Ungar, M. (2020, in press). Resilience of individuals, families, communities and environments: Mutually dependent protective processes and complex systems. In M. Ochs, M. Borcsa, & J. Schweitzer (Eds.), *Linking systemic research and practice—Innovations in paradigms, strategies and methods.* European Family Therapy Association Series, Volume 4. Cham: Springer International.

Crittenden, P. (2008). *Raising parents: Attachment, parenting and child safety.* Portland, OR: Willan Publishing.

Dallos, R., & Draper R. (2015). *An introduction to family therapy: Systemic theory and practice* (4th ed.). Maidenhead: Open University Press.

Elgot, J. (2019). NHS needs more compassionate working culture.... *The Guardian.*

Figley, C. R. (1995). *Compassion fatigue and vicarious trauma disorder in those who treat the traumatized.* New York: Brunner/Mazel.

Figley, C. R. (2008). *The compassion requirement: Overcoming the costs of caring.* Lecture at Queens University of Technology, Brisbane, Australia (personal communication).

Figley, C. R., & Nash, W. P. (2007). For those who bear the battle. In C. R. Figley & W. P. Nash (Ed.), *Combat stress injury.* New York: Routledge.

Freudenberg, H. (1974). Staff burn-out. *Journal of Social Issues, 30*(1), 159–165.

Gorvett, Z. (2019, June 11). The WHO has redefined burnout as a syndrome linked to chronic work stress .... *BBC Global News* website.

Hanks, H., & Stratton, P. (2007). On learning from the patience. *Clinical Child Psychology and Psychiatry, 12*(3), 341–347.

Hanks, H., & Vetere, A. (2016). Working at the extremes. In A. Vetere & P. Stratton (Eds.), *Interacting selves.* New York: Routledge.

Hobbs, C. J., Hanks, H. G. I., & Wynne, J. M. (1999). *Child abuse and neglect: A clinician's handbook* (p. 165). London: Churchill Livingston.

Hutchinson, E. (2019, February). We're only human after all. *The Psychologist.*

Lyth, I. M. (1988). *Containing anxieties in institutions: Selected essays.* London: Free Association Books.

Maslach, C., & Leiter, M. (2008). Early job predictors of job burnout and engagement. *Journal of Applied Psychology, 93,* 489–512.

Masson, O. (1990). le syndrome d'equisement professional: burnout. *Therapie Familiale, 11*(4), 355–370.

Obholzer, A., & Roberts, V. Z. (1994). *The unconscious at work: Individual and organisational stress in the human services.* London: Routledge.

Reeves, D. (2019, May). Workplace bullying and fairness. *Clinical Psychology Forum* (317).

Samra, R. (2012, January). Brief history of burnout. *BMJ.* https://doi.org/10.1136/bmj.k5268.

7

Long-Term Supervision in Groups: Opportunities and Challenges of a Language-Systemic Approach

T. K. Lang

Introduction

"It is fun to watch professionals work. They have so many interesting tools. You can learn a lot." A friend said this as we watched utility company workers trimming tree branches entangled with power lines. The experience reminded me of working with professionals in long-term supervision groups. Specialists in any profession develop unique ways of doing their work through years of practice. There is a lot to be learned through sharing and reflecting on this experience. In this chapter, I show how long-term supervision groups offer professionals a particularly well-suited context for reflecting dialogically on their practice, learning from it together with other professionals, and through this being confirmed as belonging to their profession.

T. K. Lang (✉)
Associate Professor of Theology, Oslo University, Oslo, Norway
e-mail: tk-lang@online.no

© The Author(s) 2020
A. Vetere and J. Sheehan (eds.), *Long Term Systemic Therapy*,
Palgrave Texts in Counselling and Psychotherapy,
https://doi.org/10.1007/978-3-030-44511-9_7

A Non-expert Approach to Supervision: A Dialogic Paradigm

As professionals, we are connected to other persons, to our professional field, and our professional past through continuously ongoing dialogue, in particular, a dialogue in the form of questions and answers. Therefore, an approach to supervision based on "a *philosophy of language*" (Wittgenstein 1953; Gadamer 1975; Ricoeur 1984, 1992) and "*dialogism*" (Buber 1970, 2002; Holquist 2002; Bakhtin 1984) has shown itself to be particularly useful. Such an approach is also founded on the firm conviction that "*the other is a stranger*," not reducible to a category (Levinas 1991), and that *truth* presupposes an agreement between at least two people, i.e., a "We" (Jaspers 1953; Gergen 1994). This awareness of the "otherness" of the other (Friedman 1976) together with a critical stance reflected in "an awareness of the power relations hidden within the assumptions of any social discourse" (Hoffman 1992, p. 22), is what prevents the dialogic supervisor from becoming monologic. It also precludes that the supervisor—disguised as an expert—directs and makes choices for the one seeking supervision.

Since the mid-1980s, I have worked with a group of supervisors developing a language-systemic mode of supervision (Anderson and Goolishian 1988; Anderson 1997) offering professionals long-term supervision in groups. While some changes have occurred over the years on account of members moving in or out of the local or professional community, several members of these groups have followed each other closely through the years, some nearly throughout their entire professional career. Notably, the latter has been the case with physicians in private practice and ministers working in a specific geographical area for most of their professional life. Others participate for as long as they occupy the professional position that makes participation relevant.

Regardless of which professional group members belong to, they express how the group has been of decisive importance to them—for some even a precondition—in accepting a particular job or being able to stay in it, particularly while working through critical periods or demands.

Much Like Peer Reviews

The supervision groups concern the members´ work situation and function much like peer reviews function when one is writing articles for professional journals. By narrating one's daily work and reflecting upon this narrative together with the group, one seeks to become the best version of oneself as a professional.

The group works through listening; recounting the story told, and then reflecting on it. Reflection takes the form of asking critical-analytical questions from a not-knowing position, sharing one's own relevant experiences, giving constructive feedback, and engaging in dialogues searching for the most professional way of doing what the narrator needs to do, or retrospectively, obviously should have done. All this time, the emphasis is on staying within the shared narrative, focusing specifically on the presentation of the story, particular words, and phrases used. To listen and remember what has been said is discovered to be a real challenge for many. Consequently, they make notes as the story unfolds, preventing them from forgetting or being seduced by their interpretations of what they have heard, thus enabling them to recount verbatim the story told. At times, groups may look much like a press conference. When this occurs, it is vital that the supervisor is an attentive listener, providing the narrator with eyes to look into as he or she talks. In general, one ignores language in favor of the issue at hand. Not so here.

The group's intention, in all this, is to clarify the narrator's professional understanding and perspective on matters in his or her professional practice. Here the group works following Heidegger's (1971) assertion that we do not know what we mean before we hear ourselves say it. In reality, he claims, we "see" with our ears because it is the language which brings everything to our awareness. Consequently, according to Heidegger, to think is to listen. Long-term supervision groups function, one may say, much like fitness centers where one instead of exercising the body is training to listen and be in that which has been said, in such a manner that the narrator can see and understand what the narrative tells. The group is interested in the narrator's comportment and attitude toward the intentional content that is being conveyed, in the philosophical and ethical stands and demands that are becoming visible through the story told, and in the manner of expression.

Both intellectually and personally this is a demanding exercise, utterly dependent on group members trusting each other. Members need to know that what is said or done in the group, stays in the group, that whatever response is given or received is offered with the other's best in mind. By trusting this, group cohesion develops fast, and the group members can concentrate their full energy on being resources for each other.

In this form of long-term supervision, we tap into the individual's life-long personal learning process and integrate this abundant resource of knowledge and skills into an interpersonal learning network of professionals. A *social internet* among professionals, one might say— alternatively, an ecology of ideas or "minds," to use Gregory Bateson's language (1972, p. 339).

An Example

Erik is a child protection entrepreneur. He and his closest staff and team leaders constitute a supervision group that meets every 4th week for two hours. Coming to one of the sessions, Erik asks if he may take up some time on this particular day. He says he wants to reflect on: "What kind of leader am I?" "What kind of leader do I want to be?" "And maybe the answers to those two questions do not coincide?" The group gives him the floor.

He shares a story about how he and one of the team leaders had been in a conversation where it became relevant that the team leader responded thus: "Well, Erik, you're not one particularly caring leader. However, you are available. Lisa is a very caring leader. She, for example, knows the names of all her employees' children. Yes, even their pets' names she remembers."

Erik wanted to reflect together with the group on, as he phrased it: "Have I become a less supportive leader? One who wants structure and professionalism, and only comments when something ain't good enough?" He then told the group that he was a member of a choir. On one occasion he had been elected to be the soloist at a concert. During their many practices preparing for the concert, the choir director not once commented on his singing. Erik had felt so bad about it, feeling he lost quite a bit of his self-confidence as a result of not knowing if what he did was right or not, in the conductor's eyes. He used this as an example of what kind of leader he did not want to be but was worried about having become, after having gotten the team leader's response. Such was the narrative he presented to the group and wanted reflections on. How reflections are done, will be addressed later.

The Groups

The oldest one of my groups, a group of physicians in private practice, has been running for 33 years, meeting 90 minutes every second or third week except for two months in the summertime and one month around Christmas. Through the last three decades I have been running, on average, some thirty groups like this each year. The timeframes for their meetings vary, depending on the frequency with which they meet, which again depends on the geographical distances they have to travel to attend.

These groups are "open groups," (Yalom 1975) admitting new members as old members either retire, move from the area, or for other reasons end their participation. They are also "work groups" (Bion 1974), groups that are meeting for a specific task, in this case, for supervision. Their organization and structure give stability and permanence to the group.

Some groups are "*mono-professional groups*," e.g., groups of physicians in private practice, principals in local schools, ministers, family therapists, supervisors, and different health- and social care professionals. While others are "*multi-professional groups*." Others again are "*transprofessional groups*" where whole staffs of institutions participate; or a department staff; a church staff; or psychologists, psychiatric nurses, social workers, family therapists, and milieu therapists working as a team in different community-based "low-threshold programs" helping families, battered or sexually abused women and men, mentally ill people and drug addicts.

If the group members have to travel far to meet, they may attend entire days like once in February, once in April and once in June, and likewise two or three times in the fall. Others may choose to meet three hours once a month, and so forth according to what fits the participants best.

A Contract Defines the Context

All these different groups have as foundations the same "*moral contract*" between the group members and the supervisor, and between the group members themselves. It defines the context— the group's organization and structure—within which the supervision takes place. It describes in detail how each group session will proceed; the philosophy behind this way of working; and the obligations of the participants over against each other and toward themselves.

Establishing the rules of procedure and presenting the philosophical stance characterizing this form of supervision as a dialogical and collaborative process, is a precondition for the work. The groups are highly organized and the meetings efficient.

Though, the supervisor's responsibility in constituting the group and the supervisory process emphasizes, the group organization and structure need to be understood as "the product of co-operation between members of the group, and their effect once established in the group is to demand still further co-operation from the individuals in the group" (Bion 1974, p. 122).

"How?" "Why?" and "Who?"—The Necessity of a Deep, Reciprocal, Shared Understanding

It is a truism in this way of thinking that real communication between participants in a conversation will only take place where there is a deep, reciprocal, and shared understanding of who the participants are:

Who are you? Who am I? What are we doing together? Why are we doing this (Gadamer 1975)? Therefore, the first session always starts with an introduction of the participants. How the group will work, and why. Making sure that the supervisor's assumptions about his or her role coincide with those held by the participants in the group, and vice versa: that the expectations about what it means to be a member of the group coincide with the expectations of the other members of the group, including the supervisor (Berger 1963).

In the introductory phase of a group I often include telling about the three most determining elements when realtors price a property: "*Location. Location. Location.*" Then I add: "When you work professionally with people, there are three equally crucial elements: *Context-defining. Context-defining. Context-defining.*"

When the context is understood and mutually agreed upon, each member of the group knows the "*rules*" that will apply in the group setting. So, the "*play*" may begin.

The Group as a Language Game

Wittgenstein (1953) introduces the analogy between game and language to underline that language includes activity, action. A language game is a section of the language and the activities into which it is interwoven. To understand a concept, Wittgenstein maintains, is to participate in a life form. Learning to master a broader human reality. If one wants to play, one needs to enter the game and participate in it. In this sense, a supervisory session is like a language game. One needs to master it to understand it. To understand the concept: "a language-systemic approach to supervision" one needs to participate in it.

"You should try it!" is a commonly expressed response the first time a group member comes back in after having been placed outside the circle with his or her back to the group. Sitting there, he or she first had to listen to the group members' verbatim recital of the story he or she just told, while sitting in the ring, facing the group. After the supervisor has asked if the story has been correctly recited, the narrator may confirm this, correct it, or add something important that has been left out.

The group members are then asked by the supervisor to reflect on the story, while the narrator still sits outside the circle with his or her back to the group making notes of thoughts that may occur while listening to the group's recitation and reflections. Thoughts that are shared and developed further, when he or she enters the circle again: "What I discovered sitting listening to my own story recited, was that …." Alternatively: "When you were reflecting on my story, I understood that…." If an entirely new story about the "real issue" occurs, the supervisor places the narrator, after having told the new story, outside the circle again with his or her back toward the group. The same procedure is then followed, as after the first story. One of the most powerful effects of this mode of supervision, is often said by the participants to be "sitting with my back towards the group and experiencing that I really have been listened to and been heard!"

The metaphor of the game is also used by Gadamer when describing how language pulls the reader of text into a meaning-universe. To the degree the reader understands what he or she reads, the reader will be drawn away by the account. The same is the case regarding the story heard told in supervisory groups, both when the group members listen to the narrated story, as well as when the narrator listens to the story recited verbatim. "In understanding, we are drawn into an event of truth and arrive, as it were, too late, if we want to know what we are supposed to believe" (Gadamer 1975, p. 484).

Entering the game's world is letting oneself be sucked into it, which changes one's position. At a certain point, the game takes over, as if one becomes part of the game itself, and ruled by it. The players follow where the game takes them.

What makes working as a supervisor so exciting is precisely this: that one never knows *what* is going to happen, or *where* it is going to lead. One only knows for sure that something *will* happen, in every session, if we "play" according to the rules. We know that no one in the group could have foreseen, planned, or manipulated this to happen. Nor would it have been possible to make it happen without the participation of these particular people in the group. The supervision group becomes a professional creative room where new insights and understanding can occur by coincidence. We experience what Bakhtin (1984), like Buber

(1970), formulated as a theory of the inter-subjective formation of the self: in revealing oneself to another, one becomes aware of oneself.

Bakhtin maintains that "Human thought becomes genuine thought, that is, an idea, only under conditions of living contact with another and alien thought, a thought embodied in someone else's voice, that is, in someone else's consciousness expressed in discourse. At that point of contact between voice-consciousnesses, the idea is born and lives" (Bakhtin 1984, p. 88). If an idea remains in one person's isolated individual consciousness only, it degenerates and dies (Jaspers 1953).

Development Within a Professional Context

The context exists first. We are born into a culture (family, local, and national), where we learn to speak, think and act, so that we become part of that culture.

In the same manner, we have studied, learned the language, and worked our way through practice, into mastering the way to do things as they are seen to be scientifically or professionally correct to do, within the science or profession to which we belong.

After entering a profession through its initiating processes, it is a condition for maintaining one's professionalism that one participates in close communication with other professionals. Supervision groups offer the possibility of doing this. Since understanding is never-ending and professional knowledge is fresh produce these groups provide a dynamic and viable knowledge arena throughout the members' entire professional lifecycle.

As a place for sharing, truthfully, stories about how one works, these groups function as a tool for securing the quality of one's daily practice through letting others "peek over one's shoulder" to see how one works; asking questions about what they "see;" giving support, corrective, or applause when appropriate. Following Bakhtin (1984, p. 287), we can never really see ourselves, and can only get an authentic image of ourselves reflected in the other's eyes. He considers the other's gaze as a precondition for the person having a sense of self at all. Subscribing to this view, we consider having other professionals' gaze on oneself as necessary for any professional to have a professional self.

One's "professional I" requires a "professional You": someone who can see me and acknowledge me and meet me openly and honestly in a manner that makes me able to hold on to myself and my stories as well as endure being challenged, so that I might discover new understandings or ways of performing my professional practice. Supervisory groups invite this process to take place through group members' narrating, listening, and engaging in exchanges with other professionals.

"The idea is a *live event*, played out at the point of dialogic meeting between two or several consciousnesses," states Bakhtin (1984, p. 88). Likewise, Gadamer (1986/1993, p. 108) emphasizes understanding as an event—as something happening to us, not something we do or achieve alone.

The group conversations lead the participants to places they never knew existed. Spontaneously an idea takes shape, is born and begins to live, becomes a live event in which the group members participate and understanding happens.

What one is witnessing then is what Hannah Arendt (1958) described as the creation of "a residue" or "a surplus." That which remains after the group session. The real product of the meetings is not what has been said or done in that encounter, but the narrative, the story that will be told afterward about what happened. That is the real product. "Oh, now I understand, and I know what I want to do!"

Alternatively, expressed in typical feedbacks like: "I was just about to say this to my client, but then I could hear your voice, TK, as if you were sitting on my shoulder talking to me, asking about my intentions in saying that which I was about to say."

The most substantial impact of language-systemic supervision comes precisely from this: the group members' voices become part of the individual member's self-reflection. Like Bakhtin said, "We are the voices that inhabit us" (Bakhtin 1981). As he argued, "it is precisely the individual utterance that should be made the central object of enquiry because it is there that the voices of self and other engage in an ongoing power struggle over meaning" (Chapman and Routledge 2005, p. 25; Bakhtin 1986, p. 89).

The Core of Supervision: Becoming a Reflective Subject in One's Professional Practice

This self-reflective inner dialogue—before, during, or after our professional encounter with our clients—is the core of supervision. It is related to what is called conscience (Latin: con-scientia, to know together with). One knows together with one's self. However, also together with others, whose voices may participate in one's inner polyphonic conversation with one's self.

Conscience shows itself as an afterthought, a reflection on thoughts and on what has been said and done. It functions as a corrective to one's future actions. Supervision functions likewise, nurturing inner conversations as afterthoughts: being about to act, one may hear voices from a supervisory session which guide one directly, so one knows what to do, or indirectly by making one anticipate reflections in a future session.

Zygmunt Bauman elegantly formulates this anticipation:

> Lives lived and lives told are for that reason closely interconnected and interdependent. One can say, paradoxically, that the stories told of lives interfere with the lives lived before the lives lived have been lived to be told. (Bauman 2001, p. 16)

This interaction between lives and stories seems to be intrinsic to our human nature. In a broader context, it also means that a human being is fundamentally social and socially interdependent. Stories and lives complexly interact with each other forming a social setting (Lang and Tysk 2017; Bateson 1972).

Critical Analysis of Professional Issues: The Group as a Language System

Such a social context is what supervision groups constitute. For as long as group members bring up themes, concerns, problems, situations, or questions from their professional work that the group finds interesting and meaningful to talk about and reflect on, the group continues to exist. In the language of Goolishian and Anderson (1987, 1988), this is what makes the supervision groups into "language systems." If they do not have issues to reflect on, the language system—created by the conversation around an "issue"—dissolves.

It is, usually, more beneficial to have multi-professional groups. By bringing forth a greater multitude of perspectives on an "issue," it more easily dissolves as a "problem." Viewed from different perspectives, an "issue" may seem irrelevant, or ways to deal with it may occur as obvious, quite different from how it does in a group of exclusively highly specialized professionals within the same field. In mono-professional groups, one experiences more often than in multi-professional groups that members think they understand too quickly. Then they easily end up talking about issues in a manner Wittgenstein describes thus:

> "The general form of propositions is: This is how things are."—That is the kind of proposition that one repeats to oneself countless times.
>
> … A picture held us captive. So we could not get outside it, for it lay in our language and language seemed to repeat it to us inexorably. (1953, §§ 114–115)

Of course, this is always a danger in conversations. As Harlene Anderson cautions, "Be tentative with what you think you might know. Knowing interferes with dialogue: it can preclude learning about the other, being inspired by them, and the spontaneity intrinsic to genuine dialogue" (2007, p. 40).

Supervision as a Reflection on Practice

I define *supervision* as "*reflection on practice*." *Practice*, in its turn, I understand with Wittgenstein (1953, §§ 202) as "*a rule plus the applying of the rule*." Which in everyday professional language would be approximate: "My *professional practice* is what I do in every instance of my professional work, as a consequence of my training, doing what is the right thing to do, within that particular context."

One cannot follow a rule "privately." One needs to be trained to follow it, as one analogically is trained to follow an order. To *believe* that one is following the rule is not to follow the rule but to act on an interpretation. Consequently, any professional will have to belong to a professional community that verifies that their practice is following "the rule," what is right to do, within that professional field of knowledge.

So what is brought to supervision is a narrative of what happened in a particular situation during a professional's everyday work—something that did not make sense, or something so challenging that the professional's self-confidence is at stake, experiencing shaking of one's professional foundations as they are threatening to lose their meaning.

The supervision functions, then, as an inquiry into the professionals' understanding ("the rule") of what they are doing or intend to be doing when they do what they do in their practice and reveal in their telling about it. Moreover, the group looks at the way things have been done or said ("the application of the rule"), to see if this meets the standards of the profession, as an adequate response to whatever the situation demanded.

Long-term supervision in groups brings, unavoidably, into discussion the concepts and understandings of the particular field of knowledge within which the professional has his or her training. Are these concepts and beliefs adequate and helpful in the actual situation about which the narrator is concerned? Scrutinizing experiences from practice that turn out *not* to be satisfying, even though one has done what one usually does in "such situations," may reveal information that will make a difference to the narrator's future practice. In this sense, our groups offer a "*tool*" or a "*room*" for an active investigation through critical analysis of the validity of one's own profession's self-evident, or axiomatic understandings. Accordingly, one's supervisory group becomes an active participant in developing the professional field to which one belongs.

Outside the Hamster Wheel

Long-term supervisory groups offer professionals a place outside their daily "hamster wheel" of running their everyday practice, continually trying to keep up with an often overwhelming amount of work and demands. The groups provide a viewpoint allowing a necessary, transcendent perspective on everyday practice, making possible the exploration of one's practice in depth in order to provide new insights. Thus, these groups become a field of knowledge creation as well as a continuous evaluation process providing quality assurance—an ongoing integrative process that may widen the group members' horizon, however, only by overturning an existing perspective as erroneous or too narrow.

Given the hermeneutic challenges in any human dialogue, it is demanding to be a supervisor with this philosophical approach. One needs to be highly aware that speech always contains more than can be immediately perceived even though the narrator both leaves a picture of him- or herself, as well as is personally present in his or her speech (Lévinas 1991). "People are what they say, but not what they say that they are." (Skjervheim 2002, p. 230). They are also their image, i.e., what they who meet them, say they are. When reflecting what has been heard and seen it is important to remember that the supervisor is not there as a specialist to criticize or correct the ones asking for supervision. Also, it is important to remember that their narrative—though revealing themselves—is about a situation where they did as best as they could at that moment. Finally, essential to have in mind is how telling about something that one is not satisfied with having done, is a daring and often scary thing to do. The supervisor has to watch out—"not so much that what you're saying is true, but that the person you're talking to can stand the truth" (Seneca, 4 BC-65, 3.36.4). Because of this one has to be very particular about how one starts the groups.

Laying Down the Foundations: The First Meeting in Detail

At the opening of the first session, each participant is asked to introduce him- or herself by name and in his or her professional capacity. Do they have any specialized education? If so, from where; and when; and what kind of specialist competence did they acquire by that? What kind of professional work experiences do they have? Where? For how long?

They are also asked to say something about their experiences with supervision and with participating in "a group like this one." If they have experience, was it good or bad? If good, what made it so? If not good, what made it so?

Finally, they are asked to say something about their expectations, here and now, at the start of their participation in this particular group.

If it is the upstart of an entirely new group, the supervisor usually starts the "introduction round" by introducing him- or herself, thus setting the standard. If it is an ongoing group, including new members, same procedure is followed plus the old members share, how long they have been in it; how they use it; and their experience of the group's value in their professional life.

The groups always sit in a circle. No table. There may be coffee, tea, and water together with cups and glasses standing on the floor in the middle of the circle.

The way the group will be working; the philosophy this work is based on; and a minute presentation of the contract that defines the group members' way of relating to each other, comes next. Often, during this presentation, old members express how they suddenly understand the importance of why we do things the way we do. Saying this, they sustain and develop the cohesiveness of the group and the group culture per se. Establishing the ground rules for the group's work together gives the supervisor as well as participants the freedom to act in whatever situation that might occur during a group session.

Fundamental to making supervision a secure "room" is the group members pledging confidentiality concerning what others are sharing in the group. What one finds out about oneself and how this affects one's further life as a professional, one may share with whoever. However, who said what in the group that made one see things differently, stays in the group. "Yours is yours. Do whatever with it. What belongs to others' stays in the group." If it is a group of co-workers making up the supervisory group, it is important to make rules, particularly about how the participating manager will not call anyone in "on the carpet" for something shared in the group. Also important to emphasize is that nothing brought into supervision becomes the leader's responsibility to handle before the one bringing it forth in the group brings it to the leader out-side the group. Sounds maybe complicated, but in practice, it turns out to be no problem.

The contract also contains an agreement on time-frame, frequency, meeting place, dates, what kind of issues are relevant to bring forth, how one ends participation, how one includes new members, and how once a year a session is set aside for evaluation. At the annual evaluation, each member evaluates his or her use of the group, how the group has been essential and shares thoughts on how each member, mentioned by name, has contributed positively in that member's perspective during the past year. Attending the group is also agreed to be a top priority commitment, in the sense that only sick-leave, vacation, and emergencies may justify absence.

If it is a 90-minutes group, I always make sure that I have at least 40 minutes at the end of the first session, asking one of the members to "jump into it" so that the group may experience a real supervisory session, learning by doing in the Wittgensteinian tradition of "meaning equals use."

The first meeting always has the same structure. Being pragmatic and not wishing to spend too much time introducing new members, we usu-ally include them in the upstart meeting after summer- or Christmas breaks.

Long-term supervision groups provide a unique context, making con-versations in that space very different from those in staff meetings, at nursing stations, or among colleagues, friends, and people in general. The difference lies in the quite particular and clearly defined frame, referred to as *the contract*: the mutual commitment to the collaborative work this form of supervision demands.

Trusting the Structure and the Process: The Format of Each Session

Each session starts with feedback from the previous session, either con-cerning the issues dealt with, what it might have led to, or how it was to attend. Then each member of the group addresses the supervisor's question: "What are you concerned about today?" While answering this question briefly, the group agrees on who is "to get time today." Groups differ in whether they decide this ahead of or at the beginning of each session.

The one who "gets the time" then tells his or her narrative concerning a job- or professional field-related theme. After that, the narrator turns his or her chair, placing him- or herself outside the group-circle with his or her back toward the group. The story told is then recited verbatim by the group members, starting with someone reciting the first part of the story, followed by the person sitting next to him or her taking up the story from where the former group member left off, and so forth until the whole story has been retold. The supervisor then asks the narrator whether the group has correctly reiterated the narrative. If things need to be corrected or added, one does so. The group then shares, in the same manner, going around the circle, what thoughts the narrative has evoked, own experiences, or relevant material from the professional field, possibly, also adding short reflections on other group members' reflections.

The narrator is then invited back into the circle to share thoughts, understandings, or insights evolving or gained while listening to the recitation and reflections. If interesting new perspectives emerge, or a story about "what the real issue is," the same procedure is followed, placing the narrator outside the circle again while the group recites and reflects on the new material presented. How many times the narrator is placed outside the group depends on what new statements may occur worth reflecting on in that way.

Back in the circle again, the narrator reports to the group, initiating dialogues within the group that may bring forth new understandings and suggestions relevant to new practices. In this last phase of the session, experience has shown how group members easily fall back into monologues and argumentative modes of communicating, losing focus on the narrator's story and issue. Consequently, it is vital that the supervisor actively upholds the dialogical and reflecting conversation with a focus on what may be useful to the one "having the time." The narrator always gets the last word before the designated time is up, or the session ends.

What Has Experience Taught Us?

First and foremost: it works.

This kind of supervision in long-term groups gives professionals working alone the experience of belonging to a professional fellowship; it also ensures the quality of their professional work, keeps them up to date within their professional field, and functions as a unique safety net when times get rough. "I wouldn't have stayed in this job of mine if it hadn't been for this group," is a commonly expressed sentiment.

In addition to the group being essential in any individual professional's life, experience with this form of supervision also reveals how whole teams or staffs at institutions often benefit from it. The teams' professional awareness is typically strengthened. The same goes for their willingness to accept both individual and collective responsibility toward clients, colleagues, and others with whom they cooperate, as well as their willingness to accept the limits and possibilities of their resources.

The culture of the long-term supervision groups, as presented in this chapter, tends to influence the culture of the whole department or institution. After a while, the culture of the group seems to set the standard also for how people communicate respectfully with each other in other encounters as well. Colleagues are paying attention to each other in quite a different way and are collaborating more efficiently because they understand and trust each other more after having shared openly with each other in the supervision group. The culture of dialogue—the training in listening and in being-in-what-is-said—that the supervisory groups develop affects how the professionals engage with other agencies and particularly how they interact with clients, patients, and significant others. As expressed by the leader of four homes for traumatized single teenage refugees at the annual evaluation after ten years of gathering for 90 minutes every two weeks (except for summers and Christmas holidays): "These supervision groups are the glue in our organization."

Conclusion

Throughout this chapter, I have emphasized the decisiveness of the contract on which this form of supervisory work depends. The moral commitment the contract implies enforces strong group cohesiveness, making it possible for the members to focus their full energy on being resources for each other and talking freely and sharing truthfully in a dialogical manner in the groups. Through this sharing of professional reflections, new understandings may emerge unexpectedly, not as something provided by a supervisor acting as an expert, nor as the result of a specific task performed by the individual, but as *an event* in which the group members are themselves, active participants.

Many people's tendencies to be self-centered, defensive, and afraid of living transparently and revealing themselves to others, are counteracted by the form of long-term supervision groups described here. The monologue of self-centeredness is transformed (or at least challenged) by the dialogical structure of the group. In the best of cases, individuals are freed from the confines of their single-minded habitual self-understandings as professionals and empowered to regard themselves anew through a plurality of available perspectives.

The concept "groupthink" from the group dynamics tradition comes to mind at this point as a challenge or warning. Irving Janis's studies of "the poor decision-making strategies used by groups responsible for such fiascoes as the Bay of Pigs invasion, the defense of Pearl Harbor before its attack in World War II, and the escalation of the Vietnam War," concludes that "in-group pressures" made these groups "the victims of *groupthink*," resulting in "a deterioration of mental efficiency, reality testing, and moral judgment" (1972, p. 9). This is why the supervisor in long-term supervision groups emphasizes, again and again, that: "Yes, this is one way to look at it. How may it look from other perspectives?"

I hear myself time and again assert that: "We don't get our life in order before it is placed in a narrative. The hope lies in that it is a good story!" Moreover, as this chapter has shown, I agree with Jaspers, who maintained that "the truth begins first where two are together" (1972, p. 93), and with Ricoeur underscoring how "we tell stories because in the last analysis human lives need and merit being narrated" (1984, p. 75). Or as the American essayist, Joan Didion writes: "We tell ourselves stories in order to live" (1979, p. 11). These stories, of course, can be both liberating and destructive forces in people's lives. The author Maggie Nelson writes that:

> I became a poet in part because I didn't want to tell stories. As far as I could tell, stories may enable us to live, but they also trap us, bring us spectacular pain. In their scramble to make sense of nonsensical things, they distort, codify, blame, aggrandize, restrict, omit, betray, mythologize, you name it. This has always struck me as cause for lament, not celebration. (2017, p. 155)

Wittgenstein and Heidegger had the same insight as the one Nelson expresses here; their philosophies demonstrated how language bewitches us, creating a picture that holds us captive. However, these two philosophers also saw language as an instrument of freedom, containing the power the Greeks called *poiesis*, and we call poetry. The supervisor must be sensitive to this dual potential in language; he or she must understand just how powerful stories can be, as both creative and destructive forces in a person's life. One of the aims of the supervision is to challenge destructive narratives while harnessing the creative and liberating potential in fresh perspectives.

Ultimately, the approach to supervision I have presented in this chapter rests on the firm conviction that it is only when professionals reflect collectively on their practice that they become truly professional. It is only through the gaze of other professionals that they come to understand who they are or should be as professionals. However, the responsibility for the person I show myself to be, in what I say or do, is never the group's responsibility. The responsibility for my responses to others, and for my answers to whatever the actual situation calls for, is mine alone.

References

Anderson, H. (1997). *Conversation, language and possibilities: A postmodern approach to therapy*. New York: Basic Books.

Anderson, H., & Gehart, D. (Eds.). (2007). *Collaborative therapy*. New York: Routledge.

Anderson, H., & Goolishian, H. (1988). Human systems as linguistic systems: Evolving ideas about the implications for theory and practice. *Family Process, 27,* 371–393.

Arendt, H. (1958). *The human condition*. Chicago, IL: The University of Chicago Press.

Bakhtin, M. M. (1981). *The dialogic imagination: Four essays by M. M. Bakhtin* (M. Holquist, Ed. and C. Emerson & M. Holquist, Trans.). Austin, TX: University of Texas Press.

Bakhtin, M. M. (1984). *Problems of Dostoevsky's poetics*. Minneapolis, MN: University of Minnesota Press.

Bakhtin, M. M. (1986). *Speech genres and other late essays* (C. Emerson, Trans. and Ed.). Minneapolis, MN: University of Minnesota Press.

Bateson, G. (1972). *Steps to an ecology of mind*. New York: Ballentine Books.

Bauman, Z. (2001). *The individualized society*. Cambridge: Polity Press.

Berger, P. (1963). *Invitation to sociology*. New York: Anchor Books.

Bion, W. R. (1974). *Experiences in groups*. New York: Ballentine Books.

Buber, M. (1970). *I and thou* (W. Kaufman, Trans.). New York: Charles Scribner's Sons.

Buber, M. (2002). *Between man and man*. New York: Routledge.

Chapman, S., & Routledge, C. (Eds.). (2005). *Key thinkers in linguistics and the philosophy of language*. New York: Oxford University Press.

Didion, J. (1979). *The white album*. New York: Simon & Schuster.

Friedman, M. (1976). *Martin Buber: The life of dialogue*. Chicago, IL: The University of Chicago Press.

Gadamer, H.-G. (1975). *Truth and method* (G. Burden & J. Cumming, Trans.). New York: Seabury Press.

Gadamer, H.-G. (1986/1993). *Gesammelte Werke I & II* (H. Jordheim, Trans. 2003). *Forståelsens Filosofi*. Oslo: J. W. Cappelens Forlag.

Gergen, K. J. (1994). *Realities and relationships: Soundings in social construction*. Camebridge, MA: Harvard University Press.

Goolishian, H., & Anderson, H. (1987). Language systems and therapy: An evolving idea. *Journal of Psychotherapy, 24,* 529–538.

Heidegger, M. (1971). *On the way to language* (P. D. Hertz, Trans.). New York: Harper & Row.

Hoffman, L. (1992). A reflexive stance for family therapy. In S. McName & J. G. Gergen (Eds.), *Therapy as social construction.* London: SAGE Publications.

Holquist, M. (2002). *Dialogism.* New York: Routledge.

Janis, I. L. (1972). *Victims of groupthink.* Boston, MA: Houghton-Mifflin.

Jaspers, K. (1953). *Einfürung in die Philosophie.* München: R. Piper & Co., Verlag.

Lang, T. K., & Tysk, K.-E. (2017). Reflection as the Core of Supervision. *Reflective Practice: Formation and Supervision in Ministry, 37.* journals.sfu.ca/rpfs/index.php/rpfs/index.

Lévinas, E. (1991). *Totality and infinity.* Dordrecht: Kluwer Academic Publishers.

Nelson, M. (2017). *The red parts.* London: Penguin Random House.

Ricoeur, P. (1984). *Time and narrative.* Chicago, IL: The University of Chicago Press.

Ricoeur, P. (1992). *Oneself as another.* Chicago, IL: The University of Chicago Press.

Seneca. On Anger 3.36.4 in Farnsworth, W. (2018). *The practicing stoic.* Boston, MA: David R. Godine.

Skjervheim, H. (2002). *Mennesket.* Oslo: Universitetsforlaget.

Wittgenstein, L. (1953). Philosophical investigations (G. E. M. Anscombe, Trans.). New York: Macmillan.

Yalom, I. D. (1975). *The theory and practice of group psychotherapy.* New York: Basic Books.

8

Ministering Reflectively: A Story of Two Groups

Paddy Sweeney and Martin Daly

We—Paddy Sweeney and Martin Daly, have worked, for several years with a two groups of clergy, with one group for nine years, and another for four. This work has become a long term project, but did not set out to be so. However, because the participants experienced it as valuable and we the facilitators have managed to retain an interest in it and a freshness to our approach, it has continued for a long time and may do for some time yet.

We are not necessarily arguing for the value of long term groups, but wish to inquire into the conditions that contributed to the groups being sustained over a lengthy period of time and what doing so added of value, to the experience for us and them. Obviously as the groups are still working, this places some restraints on the way in which we can write about them and how we might illustrate the workings of the groups.

P. Sweeney (✉) · M. Daly
Dublin, Ireland

M. Daly
e-mail: info@martindaly.ie

© The Author(s) 2020
A. Vetere and J. Sheehan (eds.), *Long Term Systemic Therapy*,
Palgrave Texts in Counselling and Psychotherapy,
https://doi.org/10.1007/978-3-030-44511-9_8

We informed the participants of our intention to write this article, sought their views of the experience and committed to providing them with an opportunity to read it and comment on it.

Beginnings

How did these groups arise? Paddy Sweeney invited several systemically trained practitioners together for a number of meetings to think about a possible initiative with clergy in the diocese of Dublin, an initiative that might contribute to the well being of clergy. This led to a very successful project which provided a scheme within which priests could, in a one to one arrangement with a chosen facilitator, reflect on their ministries and lives. From this scheme the idea came of having a group version, and in response to a call to those interested in such a group, twelve volunteered.

Developing a Reflective Ministry Group

When the group was formed–and was called a "Reflective Ministry Group" there were no plans other than to attempt to meet four times and then see what was best.

A preliminary meeting of the twelve was held to outline what a reflective ministry group was and what it was not, what the benefits might be, and how it would be organized and funded. It also offered the volunteers space to explore their questions and concerns.

It was explained that the planned group would be loosely based upon a practice common in the caring professions known as reflective practice. Reflective practice was described as a process through which professionals considered experiences arising from their work that perturbed them, or stirred them in some way, often because the experience had not turned out according to one's expectations. The reflective process offers a space, within which, with the help of others one can review one's usual practice, explore underlying assumptions and think of possible other ways of dealing with the situation or of acting in the future.

It was pointed out that the proposed group was not a therapy group, a study group, a prayer group a pressure/lobby group, or simply a convivial gathering for a chat. It was made clear that the facilitators, were not claiming or offering any technical expertise on the matters that would be discussed. The only expertise they claimed was in organizing and facilitating supportive conversations.

It was suggested that the benefits of involvement in reflective practice would be that one's service of parishioners could be enhanced, that greater satisfaction in ministry might be experienced and that it could promote personal well being by offering a context within which strong emotions stirred in the course of work would be dealt with, as could the impact of significant relationships on ministry and ministry on significant relationships.

Those who chose to participate were invited to commit to attending a set of four consecutive meetings, each meeting to last two hours would occur monthly. At the end of the module of four meetings a participant was free to leave, or to continue for another module. A third of the cost would be borne by the participant and the remaining amount would be supplied from Church funds, an arrangement to which Church authorities had previously agreed.

At that meeting, the volunteers explored issues to do with confidentiality, topics to be discussed and made suggestions about topics.

From the beginning, we both felt that it was essential that meeting be co-facilitated for the following reasons:

Co-facilitation provided the group with two different styles and approaches,
Enabled us to support each other and to be reflexive about our own and the other's approaches
Enabled us to be more creative than we might have been on our own,
Allowed us to be quasi- participants and observers at the same time, as we alternated with each other in these roles.

We brought similarities and differences to the proceedings. We are both priests, both trained systemically, but with very different backgrounds. Paddy is a priest of the diocese though much of his work has been other than the typical priestly duties. Martin, a member of a religious order, was headmaster of a boy's school for many years and worked as a therapist and organizational consultant from a systemic perspective. It has been really useful that one of us was "one of them" and one of us was not. One is perceived as being on the inside and one on the outside. Paddy knows the lie of the land, knows the culture among the group members, the scripts that they employ—too readily sometimes—to make sense of their experience. Martin, on the other hand, of necessity has to take up the position of a stranger, someone who doesn't have his bearings among them and can often, by his questions, defamiliarize their experience to them—and to Paddy—because it is unfamiliar to him. Between the two of us we embody that inside/outside perspective that is so intrinsic to a systemic inquiry. Having the two of us offering this difference helped them to feel able to trust, while feeling there was enough difference for it to be a safe risk.

Perhaps the difference referred to above between Paddy's familiarity with their contexts and Martin's unfamiliarity, has to be put alongside a demand that both of us faced: to defamiliarize ourselves from our own taken-for-granted ways of speaking, of inquiring, of framing things.

We endeavor to catch each other if we slip into language and categories that are too readily at hand, too easily adopted. This could be systemic language or some other modality in which one or other is well versed—or perhaps just recently imbibed at a course!—or it could be ecclesiastical language. Our mutual reflexive awareness of our language games and moves is critical for us to be able to invite the participants into such an awareness of their taken-for-granted ways of thinking and talking.

What Happened

The first set of four meetings were held, at the end of which another module took place and then the process continued to the end of that year.

At year's end a detailed review was done of all that had taken place. The feedback was very positive. One participant said that he would not continue as when he balanced the benefit for him against the time and effort investment, the pay back was not adequate. The others were all wishing to continue for another year. A selection of their comments are as follows:

- I found it a very edifying experience, completely free of cynicism.
- All involved approached the task with a positive attitude.
- A sense of companionship developed in the group.
- The atmosphere was warm, people were prepared to listen.
- We were not trying to get solutions rather we were exploring issues.
- It was an antidote to the solitariness of my life.
- I came initially out of curiosity, my expectations were not great, if it had not been good I would have dropped out, but I didn't.
- We were very upbeat.
- It was safe and secure. I learned a lot. It meant a lot to me. It answered a real need.
- There is a need for priests to have a context like this in which to talk about things that matter to them.
- It brought home to me that others have very similar experiences to me, I felt less alone, more energized.
- There was a great age range involved and as an older priest I got a great appreciation of men much younger in ministry and I became much more open to younger priests.
- The facilitation was very skilful and worked very well.
- The fact that the group was totally voluntary, facilitated its success.
- The way it was facilitated was a big factor in its success.
- The issues discussed were very real.
- There was a great level of good listening in the group, and great respect for one another.
- Although important and sensitive issues were discussed, there was a sense of trust and comfort.

At the end of that first year of operation, it was decided to continue for another year. The spirit reflected in the above comments continued to prevail and so the group continued year after year and is now in its ninth year.

Of course there have been some changes in personnel. Some participants have dropped out and others come in. When someone drops out an "exit interview" is held with the one withdrawing. The purpose of the interview is to see if there is something that is making continued membership undesirable. The main cause of withdrawal is that the participant has received a new post, at a considerable distance from where the group meets and that makes attendance very laborious. One person withdrew because of a "bad past" with a new comer to the group. Sickness and death has caused withdrawal, and some have withdrawn because they with time discovered that the group was not what they really wanted, they wanted a pastoral planning group, a spiritual direction group, or because of the group experience they felt emboldened to take up a one-to-one reflection process.

Nobody has made any criticism of the way the group operates, of the behavior of the other participants or the behavior of the facilitators.

Further Developments

After the first five years the members felt that what they were experiencing should be made available to others. They wrote a letter to all their fellow clergy describing their reflective ministry group and inviting new applicants. The following is an extract from the letter circulated,
"Dear Colleague
For several years now we have been participants in a group that meets to reflect upon our ministry and our lives. Some of us have been doing this for that past five years, others for a little less. These groups are part of what is known as the Ministering Reflectively project.

We have met eight times each year, --- on a weekday from 2 --- 4 pm. Our facilitated meetings have focused on a wide range of topics chosen by group members. Sometimes we have discussed critical issues bothering one or more of us. At other times we explored a topic. Recent topics included "the experience of preaching," "the same sex marriage referendum," "Belief and Believing To-day"; "Creativity," "Going on as a Priest Today – Challenges and Resources"

Our discussions are guided by facilitators, who help us to think about the topics in a deeper way, and get us thinking about our thinking and how the way we think shapes our ministry and our lives.

Recently we discussed together why we have been so loyal to the group and our meetings. It is hard to put into words, but put simply it is because we feel significantly better spirited as a result of attending. The group meetings are very different from other meetings that we priests attend. We are of all ages and generations yet the meetings are extremely safe, non threatening and yet very deep. One always goes home enlightened, seeing things in new ways and from new perspectives. One goes home restored, and refreshed, continuing, in the following week to reflect on what has opened up.

This talking together in a guided way has deepened our self awareness, developed strong bonds among us, affirmed us in our identity, made us freer in ourselves, lessened our isolation and enriched our spirits.

We have long felt that many of you, our colleagues, would enjoy our meetings, benefit from them and contribute greatly to them. Do think of joining. You can give it a trial if you so wish by attending a few meetings without any obligation to continue. Do think about it, and if interested, contact any of us or Paddy Sweeney the co-ordinator……….”

There was an excellent response to that letter. Fifteen new people came forward. Four were added to the existing group and a second group was formed which is now in its fourth year of existence.

There is now some thought being given to a new recruitment and the founding of a third group.

The Meetings—Preparation, Structure, and Process

Preparation

We prepare by meeting each month for three to four hours to think about the meetings with the two groups. We reflect on the themes of the previous sessions, the personal circumstances of the men, happenings in the diocese, Church, and society, topics suggested by the participants and also our own interests. Questioning is our major tool for exploring selected topics, so once a topic is chosen we go back and forth with each other as we try to come up with initial questions and tease out our use of language in doing so, how that would be received and particularly the kinds of responses we might expect to get, which recursively effects how we then think about the questions. This recursive relationship between the questions we consider asking and the responses we expect leads us to think of how we can ask our questions in unfamiliar ways so as to invite fresher modes of inquiry and hopefully novel responses from among the men. This process between us has kept us interested and kept them thinking anew about the familiar. It is more than a joint curiosity, it is a joint endeavor to defamiliarize ourselves with our ways of approaching themes and to demand of each other that we not become wedded to our ways of thinking, but constantly ask: is there another way we could pose that question?

We believe in interrogating any essentialist thinking. *How we think about something changes that something.* What we endeavor with the groups is to get them thinking differently about their lives and work and to think about the difference in their thinking that makes the difference.

We would describe what we are doing as a reflexive inquiry into their practice of living. This notion of practice enables us to include their work, their professional and personal relationships, their families of origin, their relationship with the organization that is more than an organization to them i.e., the Church and a range of other contexts that constitute their lives. Our hypothesis is that this inclusive focus on their practice of living has meant that the group has an ongoing task and purpose in contrast to other groups of which they might be a part or that other professionals might join for support or supervision. The task does not get completed, the learning does not end when the focus is on their becoming more reflexive in all the aspects of their lives. This hypothesis has been borne out in the feedback we received to which has been referred to above. What is critical is the kind of process we use to ensure that the inquiry into their lives has a sustained aliveness to it.

Structure and Process of Meetings

We begin meetings by briefly checking on how everyone is and by inviting anyone with a pressing concern and who would wish to have that
concern discussed, to take precedence over our pre-planned topic.

When a concern is raised or we move on to the prepared topic we
pose the question that we believe will trigger useful reflection and ask
the participants to reflect in silence or talk in groups of two for some
minutes to "get into" the topic

Participants are then invited to tell a story, that illustrates their connection with the topic.

They are asked to use a story format. We stress the story format
because we all are storytellers by nature and culture, the story format
discloses more than analytical statements, and it promotes an egalitarian
atmosphere in the gathering.

We also stress that the stories be told in everyday language, staying
very close to the teller's experience and where possible avoiding filter-
ing through constructs from psychology, theology, philosophy, or other
bodies of knowledge.

As the first participant tells his story, we invite the others to listen carefully and when the story has been told we ask the listeners to comment,
firstly to comment on how the person told the story e.g. "he seemed
very downbeat" or "he seems to be holding others responsible for his
situation."

We invite them to say where the story "takes each listener," and how
they do or do not relate to the story.

The original storyteller listens to the discussion in silence. When all
the comments have been made he then is invited to comment on what
he has heard "where it has taken him" and what he might consider as a
consequence of the experience of hearing the comments.

The meeting then moves on to hear the next story and the same process is repeated.

Often the stories of all members are heard, but not necessarily. Often
very important themes emerge, which the group wants and needs to
explore. When this occurs, we as facilitators strive to keep participants
thinking about how their "thinking," how experiences and thinking are

reflexively connected, and how different thinking might make a difference. At these times we must be vigilant and prevent participants drifting onto a well-worn paths of how the organization/diocese is to blame for their pressures and what it must do differently. We also need to prevent the discussion becoming a technical discussion about better ways of doing the task that priests must undertake.

We might also point out that when the stories are being told we as facilitators sometimes tell our stories. Our co-facilitation enables this as one can offer a story and the other remain in the position of inquirer about that and all the other stories. This creates a more collaborative spirit in the group, it also helps others to be more open and when a topic is very unfamiliar to the members, one of us will go first to offer a direction or initiate the inquiry.

Typically, time goes by very quickly, and at the end if there is some time, participants might be asked what they are taking with them from the meeting as they go home

Examining the Experience

These groups have been quite long lived and in the context of this book the questions that are of interest must be—Why have they endured? What benefits have accrued from this longevity? And what constraints and challenges have been thrown up?

In an attempt to answer these questions we decided to invite the members of the two groups to struggle with them

From the discussions the following emerged.

Participants' Reflections

Surprise

Participants noted that the meetings never become boring, and nobody ever seems to doze off at a session. They attribute this in part to the fact that the facilitators were regularly introducing unexpected topics, topics not likely to have been discussed by a groups of priests previously, topics about which members did not have ready-made comments to offer, but had to think more deeply. At other times interest is maintained because the topics dealt with involve serious challenges facing members.

It was also felt that freshness was maintained over the years by the addition of new members from time to time, yet the format and formula remained the same.

Exploration Focused

A very important factor, it was believed, was that in the group the emphasis was on exploring, not on reaching solutions, that one never knew where one was going, but that was all right, the uncertainty was safe, the confusion that could arise was stimulating rather than unnerving, that difference of perspective was a benefit, not a drawback, and that it was very interesting to see why people had the perspectives that they had.

Life Focused

It was felt that the group had endured because it had focused not just on narrow work-related matters but also in life events, particularly events being experienced by a group member e.g., sickness, death of a loved one, loss, hurt and forgiveness, difficulties with siblings. One member suggested that instead of being called a reflective ministry group, a more apt name might be "Living Reflectively." Another suggested that because living is a long term project, a group like this that focuses on living will naturally become a long term project.

Combats Isolation

There was general agreement that the longevity of the group was made possible by the level of trust that had built up, and the bonds that had emerged. In addition, the fact that the work and life of a priest could be isolated and isolating was offset in that these groups provided community and the need for community was long term.

Validation and Respect

It was pointed out that the group was probably the only professional context within which one was asked how one is, and the only professional context where there is concern for how one is. It was also agreed that the level of respect for one another, the lack of ego tripping and the skills of the facilitators made a great contribution to the fact that the groups exist after nine years and four years, respectively.

Disadvantages

When pressed to name constraints and disadvantages to long term membership of the group, nothing significant was forthcoming.

Facilitators Reflections

We as facilitators would concur with the factors named above by participants. We would however see some additional factors as being very significant.

Credibility

This project grew out of an earlier project which involved a one to one format. That format in turn grew out of Paddy's work with priests generally. Evaluations that have taken place show that the success of these projects is connected in significant ways with his credibility among priests. When probed as to what constitutes this credibility, it seems to be based on a perception of him as being committed to the well being of priests, that he has professional training and is not an establishment figure but is trusted by the establishment. Evaluations show that this credibility has enabled priests to risk partaking in schemes which he undertakes, and enables priests to take risks with others he involves, in this case, Martin.

Investment of Time and Effort

There is a tendency in society and in the Church to set up projects and then leave them to their own devices in the expectation that all will go well. This often leads to loss of energy and momentum. Sustainability requires careful and long term nurturing.

We have constantly nurtured this undertaking. A lot of time is spent in preparation, regular reviews are held so that participants' experience can be monitored. Exit interviews are held when a member leaves, the participants are included in every decision and regular reports are made to the leadership of the diocese

Co-facilitation

A major factor has been that it has been conducted by co-facilitators a factor that has been commented on above. But it must also be said that when one facilitates groups one can experience anxiety, fear, isolation, burdened. At such moments the presence of a collaborative co-facilitator is invaluable

Protection of Relationship

As has been explained already one of the facilitators is an insider and one an outsider. One consequence of that is that the insider is very conscious of the relationship between the project and the diocese, meaning the leadership of the diocese and the rank and file priests of the diocese. It is important that the wider organization and the leadership appreciate the project, support it and see it as worthwhile. This is crucial to the success of the undertaking. Support groups are a feature of many organizations and one of the significant factors as reported by (Hartley and Kennard

2009) is the relationship between the support group and the organization within which it is nested. Where that relationship is difficult, weak, or not existent support groups tend to fizzle out and/or participants begin to doubt their value.

Managed Risk

A significant factor has been that participants are invited to take small steps at a time that are manageable: no great leaps are asked for.

First, volunteers were supported by the credibility of one of the facilitators, later recruits, by the witness of existing members when they wrote the letter described above. Prospective members can come without obligation to a few meeting and leave without explanation. When a member commits, it is for one module at a time and very serious attention is given in the facilitation of meetings that no one feels cornered, disrespected, or hurtfully challenged.

At all stages there are small leaps and secure safety nets.

Benefits and Constraints

The participants have outlined already the benefits that they believe have accrued from membership of the groups. We as facilitators would concur that these have indeed been benefits, but have there been additional benefits from the fact that the groups have been long lived?

The major benefit has been the growth and change that is observable in participants over time. Growth and development cannot be rushed, and we live in a time when everything must be instant, even the growth of animals and plants are forced. When one works long term one receives surprises, suddenly at a meeting a once quiet participant becomes most articulate, another participant comes out with new ways of thinking or talking, another begins to talk differently and participate differently and one knows that the members themselves are not particularly conscious of what ways they are changing. There is really only one explanation for such sudden steps forward: the time has come and a length of time was necessary.

The second benefit is that relationships in the group and between members and facilitators shift in their quality. As time passes they become more like family relationships than workplace relationships, bonds deepen. As had been said in feedback from participants this affords great trust, greater sense of solidarity, a sense that there is someone at your back. The longer the groups exist the deeper these relationships seem to become.

A challenge that arises is the converse of all of this. As relationships become more familial can we as facilitators ever leave the group.? Yes we could leave due to illness or change of posting, but could we ever walk away just because we have had enough and of course when we think this way it immediately raises the issue if this is also a question for the members. Would some members now like to walk away, but feel guilty if they did so? Do they feel tied forever with no guilt free exit. Maybe this would be a good topic to discuss within the group. Again there is no evidence that anyone feels locked in and wants out. But it is an interesting place to have arrived at.

The other challenge is the challenge of keeping fresh, of keeping an element of unpredictability. We must keep re-inventing ourselves as a project, but is that possible and for how long?

Influences

As has been already said both of us trained as systemic family therapists and in working with the groups this is a common language for us and constitutes the basis of our approach to the task. It must be said however that we can be eclectic and will draw on other bodies of knowledge that we feel will enhance what we do.

But both of us are also very different, have different experiences, trainings, and outlooks, and are subject to different influences

For Martin an important influence has been his own experience, the experience of how certain persons responded to him and by their way of responding enabled him to delve deeper and more openly into the many layers of his world of work and family and life. He likens this experience to an apprenticeship within which he learned much that he now draws upon when we work.

Secondly, his work has been shaped by observing a number of wonderful practitioners at work: especially Michael White (2007), Karl Tomm et al. (2014), and Paolo Bertrando (2018), and particularly how they ask questions.

He has been influenced by the Milan focus on curiosity (Cecchin 1987) and irreverence (Cecchin et al. 1992), and by the work of John Byng-Hall on scripts in families and groups (Byng-Hall 1995).

Philosophically, he draws on the phenomenological tradition from Goethe, Husserl, Merleau-Ponty (Moran and Mooney 2002), and more recently a number of thinkers who locate themselves in this tradition and traverse disciplines, among whom are Tim Ingold (2011) and Henri Bortoft (2012) He thinks of the way he inquires as trying to "stay with the things themselves," the phenomena, and not to remove himself from the immediacy of experience. He sees what we do as a quasi-anthropological field work: we are trying to take seriously the intra-cultural variation in these groups and to be aware of our being both part of their culture and in the field at the same time asking questions as though we were among them for the first time.

One of the fundamental questions for all personnel who face new appointments every few years and live alone is how they attach and detach, how they form meaningful connections and cope with having to form new ones on a regular basis. This has led Martin to return to Winnicott's and others' work on attachment theory to help him think about how to find ways to explore these themes with the groups and to understand the very particular nature of their attachment to each other in the groups, their attachment to the diocese, the way they relate to the authority figures in the diocese and their relationship to facilitators.

For Paddy also, his experience and involvement in many groups has been formative. For many years he was director of a residential unit for troubled and troublesome young people and in that context had a very special concern for staff formation and support. Lessons learned in that context have been important as has being a participant in various groups over time some offering good experiences and some bad.

For Paddy the influence of the Milan approach, especially the contribution of Gianfranco Cecchin has been very telling (Cecchin 1996),

He has an strong commitment to creating a process that makes a difference for people. This raises the question as to what is our theory of change and what is its source.

His underpinning belief is that change occurs when one's way of thinking and acting is disrupted and a new way of thinking and acting must be put in place. In the meeting this disruption is achieved by inviting a multiplicity of stories and perspectives when a topic is being discussed. When stories and views are shared the mono—views of participants are very gently challenged and out of the range of views of offered each individual can generate a way of thinking about the issue that fits well for him. The individual leaves the meeting with a wider repertoire of ideas that he possessed upon arrival.

New thinking can also be generated by "doing differently." This is achieved at times by introducing the unexpected, at times by the choice of topic for discussion, at times by how the topic to be discussed is posed or by the way participants are asked to structure the discussion e.g., on one occasion in the "older group" they were asked to interview the facilitators to try to work out what their ideas were as to how to create a satisfactory process.

These ideas are rooted in the later Milan Systemic ideas, especially the ideas of Gianfranco Cecchin.

One consequence of this is that the atmosphere of a meeting is very exploratory and as was noted above this is something that is valued by the members, therefore "curiosity" is a key value, exploring how members came to believe what they believe, exploring the logic of their positions. Here again there is an indebtedness to Milan and Cecchin especially ideas set out in his paper on Curiosity (Cecchin 1987).

There are other traces of the ideas of that paper by Cecchin in the work. Cecchin saw an important connection between loss of curiosity and the experience of boredom. We the facilitators are constantly tuned in to signs of a member "fading away" from the discussion or indeed a lowering of energy in the whole group or in themselves and immediately inquire if what is being discussed is or is not useful.

Use is also made of the earlier Milan paper on Hypothesizing, Circularity and Neutrality (Selvini et al. 1980).

In that paper the therapist is advised to make hypotheses, and advised to go into a therapy session with creative hypotheses, ones that will when explored trigger fresh angles on issues. This influences a constant wish to be unpredictable. That paper stresses the importance of circularity, of building on feedback—feedback is followed in the meetings, but also in the total process, everything gets built on what the group does, when the facilitators do, what they do.

Neutrality is also characteristic of the y approach, the facilitators try to be curious, avoiding allying themselves with any position or set of ideas, although this is, at times, a challenge as one could drift into taking a psycho—educational stance with the group.

It is important that the work of the groups be an exercise in co-creation, that it is something that the facilitators do with the members, not something that they do to the members. To this end, the members are involved in all decisions, but also when a topic is being discussed the facilitators participate by offering their own stories and perspectives: in that sense, they are participant–facilitators.

An important influence for Paddy has come from watching the work of the late David Campbell and Ros Draper (1985), They saw the value of the idea of the "pilot project" as a construct and of asking people to commit to small, well-defined pieces of work at time—hence the idea of the scheme, at first, being introduced as a pilot project and the idea of asking people to commit to modules of four sessions per module

Other influences that have been drawn upon are Appreciative Inquiry, in that the focus is primarily on pluses rather than minuses in situation.

Narrative theory as enunciated by Jill Freedman and Gene Combs (2016, 2017, 2018) has offered a helpful paradigm that is easily allied with the Cecchin ideas about altering thinking and useful techniques e.g., asking someone to tell a story, then asking the others what resonates for them, where it takes the listener and later asking similar questions to the storyteller about his experience of the contributions.

Harlene Anderson and Harry Goolishan shifted family therapy away from a focus on social systems to a focus on language and linguistic systems. From a different but related perspective, the work of Foucault

(1975) on "discourses" that possess us, are approaches that are attractive to and that inform the approach as do the ideas of John Byng Hall on scripts.

The systemic world in the past twenty years has laid great emphasis upon the need for therapists and other professionals being reflexive. When we as co-facilitators have our monthly meetings we are constantly attempting to be reflexive, trying to identify what prejudices and assumptions we are bringing to the task and at our periodic reviews with the groups trying to identify the effects of what we do, on the participants.

We have described this project which has developed into a long term undertaking. We are not promoting long term projects, although we do see their value. We invite the reader having heard our story to note what strikes them in this story, to see where it takes them, and reflect on what it might get them doing.

References

Bertrando, Paolo. (2018). *The dialogical therapist: Dialogue in systemic practice.* London: Routledge.

Bortoft, Henri. (2012). *Taking appearance seriously: The dynamic way of seeing in Goethe and European thought.* Edinburgh: Floris Books.

Byng-Hall, J. (1995). *Rewriting family scripts.* New York: Guildford Press.

Campbell, D., & Draper, R. (1985). *Applications of milan systemic therapy: The milan approach.* London: Grune and Stratton.

Cecchin, G. (1987). Hypothesizing, circularity and neutrality revisited: An invitation to curiosity. *Family Process, 26,* 405–413.

Cecchin, G., Lane, G., & Ray, W. (1992). *Irreverence: A strategy for therapist survival.* London: Karnac.

Cecchin, G. (1996). *Personal communication.*

Combs, G., & Freedman, G. (2016, 2017, 2018). *Personal communications.*

Foucault, M. (1975). *The birth of the clinic.* New York: Random House.

Hartley, P., & Kennard, D. (2009). *Staff support groups in the helping professions.* London and New York: Routledge.

Ingold, Tim. (2011). *Being alive: Essays on movement, knowledge and description.* London: Routledge.

Moran, Dermot, & Mooney, Timothy. (2002). *The phenomenology reader.* London: Routledge.

Selvini Palazzoli, M., Boscolo, L., Cecchin, G., & Prata, G. (1980). Hypothesizing—Circularity—Neutrality: Three guidelines for the conductor of the session. *Family Process, 19,* 3–12.

Tomm, K., St. George, S., Wulff, D., & Strong, T. (2014). *Patterns in interpersonal interactions: Inviting relational understandings for therapeutic change.* London: Routledge.

White, Michael. (2007). *Maps of narrative practice.* New York: W. W. Norton and Company.

Part IV

Long Term Systemic Work with Family Businesses

9

Families in Business—The Longer Term Perspective

Ana Aguirregabiria

Introduction: Families in Business

Families in business together is hardly a new field; families have been together in business for millennia; children learning from their parents for example agricultural trades, and masteries like cobbler, tailor or smith.

According to the Institute for Family Business (IFB: https://www.ifb.org.uk/knowledge-hub/about-family-business/ sited 22 April 2020), two thirds of the businesses in the UK are owned by families, this represents a 88% of business trading in 2016. The IFB estimates that there are 4.8 million businesses in the UK. Over 16,000 businesses are large and medium sizes. According to the IFB family firms employ 13.4 million people, which represents 50% of private-sector employment. In summary, most businesses in the UK are owned by families and they employ

A. Aguirregabiria (✉)
DoctorAna Solutions, London, UK

© The Author(s) 2020
A. Vetere and J. Sheehan (eds.), *Long Term Systemic Therapy*,
Palgrave Texts in Counselling and Psychotherapy,
https://doi.org/10.1007/978-3-030-44511-9_9

a large proportion of the population. Evidently, families in business is far from a niche area. However, there are sector-specific challenges.

Peer reviewed information regarding this field is mostly published quarterly by the Family Firm Institute in the journal Family Business Review (FBR). The FBR started in 1988 and focuses on the dynamics of family-controlled enterprises of all sizes. The definition of "family dynamics" is broad and includes psychological and financial perspectives. I have found little information regarding this topic in other journals. It seems that we are still at the early stages of the field as to professionals treating it from the psychological and therapeutic, rather than the strategic or financial perspective. The Psychodynamics of Family Business (PDFB) originally founded by Dr Kenneth Kaye, celebrates 25 years anniversary of meetings in 2019. The organisation includes professionals from different therapeutic perspectives, mostly systemic family therapy. I have noticed that in Britain we tend to refer to psychodynamic when it relates to psychoanalytical psychotherapy. However, for our American counterparts the term dynamics of family business refers more literally to the interplay between the family and the business.

The Present Situation: Complex Dual Attachment and Relationships

Although the relationship between and among families owning businesses is ancient, there is an emerging awareness of the complex interaction between being a member of a family and owner of a business. Frequently, family enterprises are concerned by the overlapping issues that emerge from belonging to a family and a business at the same time, with different degrees of involvement and kinship. The tension between belonging and independence is one of the more commonly expressed concerns for families in these circumstances, between and across generations.

Emerging conflict in the family may lead to abrupt transitions in a business which can cause its decline. The reciprocal interaction between the family and the business makes working with this relationship itself a fundamental area of potential growth as well as tension. While the importance of human capital is very obvious for those professionals focused on the relationships between people, this may be less clear for those whose focus is on financial capital. Families are likely to express their goals for professional intervention as the promotion of growth and prosperity of the enterprise and family together, in order for both to succeed.

Many family advisors focus on the technical and mechanical aspects of running a business, ignoring the emotional and familial relational dynamics as well as the relationship of the family with the business. They provide families with answers regarding what to do in certain concrete situations. Advisors respond to questions brought up by the owners of the business. In turn, they expect owners to follow their advice. However, such advice may not always be possible for the family to follow. In those situations, greater understanding of the impact of attachment and emotional intelligence, the processes that engage relationships, helps us achieve success in both areas, business and family harmony.

Features of the Relational Work

The Longer View

The work of trusted advisors to a family business develops gradually over time. Strike (2013) illustrates in her study how the most trusted advisors work with the same family for more than a decade and sometimes over more than one generation in their specific role as solicitors, tax or finance advisors or banking experts. Families are likely to understand the value added by a trusted advisor specially when the work required to achieve their goal spans long periods of time. The perspective, as a family business, maybe focused more on longevity than on profit alone. Considering there is usually "a lot at stake" most families are likely to prefer to sort the root of the problem than to apply a "quick fix".

The work I undertake with family businesses fits this approach. Although each family has unique issues, in many situations our engagement may last months or even years. During our engagement I mindfully apply principles derived from research and clinical practice in family systems theory and others such as interpersonal neurobiology. I find that these principles contribute positively to bring about resolution and success for the families I am engaged with in longer term work.

There are additional factors that support a longer term engagement in this area:

1. The profile of family members themselves and their interrelationships;
2. The specific needs of the business and its own developmental stage;
3. Financial strains of the business and the family.

In my experience, the greater the complexity within the family system and between them and the business, the more sophisticated the work needs to be. This may translate in a more gradual and time aware approach. Planning an intervention needs to allow for the changes to be apparent as well as consolidate over time to prevent the system reverting to previous ways of relating.

The Profile of Family Members

There are families whose members are actively engaged in working hands on in their business. They may be taking leadership positions, travelling, and under time pressure to juggle numerous deadlines and commitments. This means that to achieve an identified goal with a family, our meetings need to be spaced over time. We seize the opportunity to meet when they can all be together and the number of meetings is negotiated as the work evolves. Our work together is interwoven within the family and in between the rest of their lives and obligations. For this reason, it is essential to accommodate to the needs and timings of our clients.

Frequently the family members that I meet are likely to be isolated overall, find it difficult to trust others, have a low tolerance for failure or to "wait and see". They operate better together when a concrete action plan or a solution is provided. For this reason they may find more traditional approaches to therapy less attractive, and prefer to engage in doing work that is likely to benefit the family; their business and their future in a concrete and goal-oriented way. This may mean less frequent meetings extended over a longer period of time.

Families may not seek "family therapy" as such to start with. They may formulate their goals variously as increasing cooperation skills, improving communication, resolving existing conflicts, increasing harmony in their relationships, developing greater ability to make decisions and keep calm during meetings, increasing their attention and goal-oriented behaviour, keeping conversations to the topic agreed in their agenda, improving communication, understanding the complexities involved in delegating tasks to other family members, and distinguishing that from the trust they have towards each other as relatives. I describe common misconceptions associated with trust later on in the section When Trust is a concern. In brief, families may mix the idea of trusting a family member with their views on that relative's competence on a specific task. Often families may need to review their beliefs about each other in more concrete terms, so they can free their relationships from the burden of holding on to beliefs that no longer serve them.

In our work together, there are interventions directed at developing mindsight, alignment and harmony in their relationships as well as develop skills within each individual.

When the Family Addresses Disharmony Within a Generation: Sibling Rivalry

Families may come to request our help due to disharmony present within the sibling generation that translates into a number of visible behaviours; arguments, people talking over each other or perhaps not talking at all, family members not turning up for either business meetings or family gatherings, and slow or absent progress with the plans they had originally agreed to achieve.

I have worked closely with families where the siblings distrusted each other to the point that their disharmony was affecting other professionals working with them within their company or on its board. Numerous behaviours can be distracting and unproductive in a board meeting whether verbal or non verbal behaviour. Examples include lack of eye contact with other participants, fiddling with a mobile phone, doodling excessively, lack of active contribution in meetings, disparaging comments towards the other sibling, excessive questioning of proposals when they originate from their sibling. These behaviours are easy to identify and can be demotivating for those around the family members which eventually will have an impact on the productivity as well as the morale of the whole company. Undoubtelly, this will impact the company's profitability.

Working with a particular family brought to the fore that sibling rivalry in these situations may have started from early on, when they were young children. When exploring how they developed their social skills through play they often describe playing in parallel; one had the dog the other had the swimming pool. Neither could recall examples of cooperative play, such as building together a den in the garden or making a surprise gift for their parent. They also describe games and situations that implied that one of them is the leader and the other the follower, keeping routinely to these fixed roles. For example, the younger brother getting out of bed to turn the light off at night at his older brother's command. The older brother making the first choice of toys, kept in the same trunk, while the younger brother found something else to do. The consequence was that neither of them were able to come up with stories of a time when they did something together successfully, when they made a joint decision, plan, or activity. Instead, they had many stories of how one drew a line on the floor each marking his territory and forbidding the other one from entering. In these stories, there are no adults listening to their plea, considering what is happening and how to learn to share, take turns, be in the same team coming up with a shared goal.

Any and all these stories in isolation certainly do not confirm sibling rivalry. However, together with other information they may indicate that the rivalry that was initially within the norm of siblings may have calcified. Over time the many ruptures in their relationship build up an unsurmountable rift, a relational trauma. For example, one sibling said he had noticed his younger brother had "beefed up" with physical training. As a result, he was concerned he was going to be beaten up coming in or out of meetings and avoided attending them altogether.

When the Family Faces "Hunger in the World of Plenty"

I have come to realise that mental illness specialists may find it harder to consider what is absent in an apparently affluent system that easily provides comfortable solutions for physical needs and problems. We are mostly trained to understand the impact of lack: poverty, abuse, ill health, trauma. I have not found as much training provided to understand the impact of lack when there is enough; when we face "hunger in the world of plenty" and bring compassion for the struggle that this situation may trigger for those involved. Often the same applies to the family members themselves. They present with a confusion—how come they are in this situation when they have "everything" when life "should" be easier? Finding what may be missing and identifying ways to resolve it is a substantial part of the journey.

I have found that in some of these families parents may not have been actively involved in the daily care giving of their children, having employed professional care givers instead: nannies, guardians, tutors and drivers. These care givers may have provided a caring, consistent and stable relationship with the child, smoothing the way of small inconveniences that may arise in life. Being easily ready in the morning, at school on time, homework completed. Loving parents may have delegated the evening routines to their support team, who run a tight ship, and life continues to move on smoothly; no battles to go to bed, no children reading under the covers with their torches until late. And yet, sometimes not all is entirely well. Parents still worry about the wellbeing of their children and this takes them away from their duties.

I have come across examples of families preparing to hand over ownership of the their business to the next generation. This is a busy period full of significant decisions to be made on behalf of the second and third generation and those who may follow on. The current generation may be stretched working in the business and sorting the administration maze that this change brings. In one case, a loving parent was proud of John, their resourceful 6-year-old son, attending both "big school" and his favourite after school club. After school, a driver would pick John up and take him to swimming club. In the meantime, his parents were busy at work. However, on the way to his after school club John would get distressed and request the driver to call his mother. She was busy in a scheduled meeting at that time. John persuaded his driver to make the call by explaining that he wanted to ask his mother for permission to eat two sweet biscuits rather than his usual one biscuit, that came in his snack bag. Once in a call with his mother John would cry and ask his mother to send him back home. This conversation would last for some-time, and his mother found herself trying to convince him to continue on his way to swimming club, have two sweet biscuits and stop crying. Negotiations would ensue to encourage John to continue his day. These conversations were distressing for both and mum was not able to fully understand what was wrong for her son and was herself under pressure to complete the call quickly and return to her meeting.

During our conversation the mother realised how important it was for her son to touch base with his mother after school, while on his way to the club. We figured that the call was addressing an attachment need to connect with his mother, to touch base before moving on to his next activity. The comfort of the circumstances was not enough to meet his emotional need for connection. The mother was able to make the connection between her and her son, to change in order to provide for this need for connection. She was also able to reflect on how different the situation was for her as a child. Her relationship between her and her parents, the first generation of the family business. Her parents were too busy to be able to adjust to meet her needs for connection.

From then on the mother planned ahead a daily call in her schedule while John was in the car. John enjoyed anticipating their connection as well as the brief conversation on his way to the club and was no longer teary, stopped asking for additional sweets and was glad to be driven to his club. John needed to connect with his primary attachment figure before he could engage in his next activity of the day. Once that need was met then he was able to face the world again with gusto. Our new gained understanding of the need to connect brought to the second generation a significant insight into their emotional needs and the potential needs of future generations. This lead to a very productive strategy to ensure that the family was able to address these needs rather than ignore them.

Giving each other time and attention became a valuable asset for them all to share.

The Specific Needs of the Business and Its Own Life Cycle

Companies go through their own developmental pathway. The life cycle of a company has been described as going through different stages, as it is conceived, created, grows and expands, and it may continue this trend or stop operating. Company owners need to adjust their business strategy to the needs of the company. When the company is owned by the family this means that the family may need to adjust themselves in order for the company to survive.

Significant transitions in the life cycle of a company are likely to bring greater need to change behaviour, strategy, finances on the owners. In turn, this can increase the pressure on the family to adapt in order to support the growth of the business. Frequently, I am requested to support families at different transition points of the business, where there may be greater pressure on the owners. The length of my engagement with the family is likely to be related to the length of the process of change of the business, as both are intricately related. I may be engaged in supporting the family create a different leadership structure, from the direction falling solely on the owner's shoulders, say the parents, to a leadership that includes the next generation as well as professionals employed to undertake specific skilled tasks such as head of human resources. The change in leadership may be planned as a next step in the development of the organisation or unplanned. In all these examples, the family may attend sessions with me not with the focus on their interpersonal familial difficulties for "family therapy" but with the dual purpose of decreasing internal conflict and improving communication, as well as guaranteeing the survival of their company.

When the Leadership Changes in an Unexpected and Unplanned Way

For example, in the case of the sudden death of the owner and main leader of the business, the family faces significant challenges. The unexpected and premature death of a business owner may leave the business temporarily without a leader and without a decision making organ. Professional business advisors are likely to take a prominent role in this situation and turn to the successors to provide advice as well as for decisions and direction. In parallel, the family may need support to go through the impact of the absence of their loved one. This situation poses unique challenges for the spouse and children, who are likely to come across information about the deceased that perhaps they were not familiar with, for example, business decisions and strategies the deceased used; the underpinning values behind these decisions becoming more apparent; the owner's vision for the future of the enterprise and wishes for their family. The wishes of a father for his older son to follow in his footsteps may come to light, while his daughter is not offered the same opportunity. Such a discovery may elicit strong feelings in the family and affect the direction of the company for a time. A parent who has left a number of unfinished transactions and no explicit strategy behind, may leave family members discussing long and hard how to proceed with these investments unless they are familiar with the values and vision of their parent.

Ideally our engagement with the family is designed to facilitate the process of change from one stage of their family life to the next. We may then be engaged in working with the family until the transition both with the business and the family life consolidates and the family feels they have arrived at a new found balance. During this process the family may come to know their husband and parent in a very different light, say a business owner may have decided to invest heavily outside the business leaving debt to be paid over time from the proceeds of the business. However, their premature death may trigger a domino effect of changes where the previous owner's plan is no longer a sound option for the next generation. Children may be left with the dilemma of deciding how to resolve this situation; complete their parent's vision and wishes to keep the investment in spite of the change in the situation, or sell the investments and direct the capital to the main business for its survival. Although this decision may appear simple from the purely financial perspective, many children may feel conflicted about selling something that their parent once owned and cherished immediately after his death. Some children may have created an attachment to the investment in the absence of their loved parent, and believe their role is to follow their parent footsteps or highly regarded vision.

The family may feel divided in their plan for the future and unable to agree on a joint way forward. Some members may wish to sell whereas others may prefer to keep the investment and finance the business in a different way. During times of stress such as these the dynamics of the family existing prior to their bereavement is likely to emerge, making it harder for them to access their communication and cooperation skills, their trust and care for each other, and their support during their bereavement.

When the Family Faces Unplanned Adjustments in Their Relationship Agreements

I was invited to join an expert team who were working to change the ownership structure of a family business. The business had grown over time and the family were advised the business capital should remain within blood lines. This approach would prevent the division of the business over time and the dilution of the ownership of the business among non-blood relative family members over future generations. Blood relatives in the family were requested by their legal advisor to approach their spouses and ask them to sign a post-nuptial agreement. In the new agreement, the in-laws were to accept new terms in case of a potential divorce or the spouse's death. The new terms meant that the in-laws would renounce ownership of any part of the family business that they might have been entitled to through marriage. The initiative was received with great reluctance in the second generation of business owners who were troubled by the potential impact of the initiative on their spouses and their relationships; not to mention the impact that this new rule could have on their children and their children's future spouses.

For this family it was very important to appreciate the distinction between being a member of the family and being a member of the business. Intense conflict arose intensely when considering their values related to ownership and membership, belonging and attachment to each other and their spouses. Our work together supported non-blood relatives in understanding and accepting the intentions behind the strategy whose purpose was to ensure the comfortable survival of their children. In addition, blood relatives had a chance to explore their own strong feelings of betrayal and abandonment that arose from "cutting their spouses out" of their "entitled" part of the business. Underneath these concerns were true worries about the family's criteria for membership; what do we need to do/be in order to belong to each other? Sometimes family members may assess membership to the family business in relation to the degree of sacrifice and devotion they show to the business itself, not necessarily each other or their relationships.

When Trust Is a Concern

Whichever specific theoretical model we use to work with we must include as a priority building trust and transparency as well as keeping in mind the three universal therapeutic factors named by Carl Rogers (1951); positive regard, acceptance and coherence. Similarly, our role working with families is to connect family, business and ownership, to be aware of both process and content, to deal with long standing complex emotions and relationships and to navigate comfortably a multidisciplinary team that may not be expert in our specific area of human capital or understand the tools we use to bring change in families. Responding to the needs of this client group requires building trust over time. To earn trust with a family means to be able to show consistently all the characteristics of a sound therapist. For example, self awareness, truth to your personal values, honesty about your opinions, competency in the areas where you provide your opinion (and similarly withhold opinion in those areas where there is no corresponding competency and defer to the expert advisor in that area). This list includes devoting individual time with each member of the core family group and the family as a whole.

Families may have difficulties navigating the complex interplay of trust in their relationships as well. According to Kaye (2010) the more roles we play in our relationship with a family the more complex it is to assess trustworthiness. In my experience, trust is potentially a misused word to indicate additional parameters for example, competency, developmental stage of the person, clarity regarding the task at hand and personal responsibility. We may trust our child to do something but they may not have the competence do do something else. Discernment is essential to build trust and clarity in the roles we play with each other.

I worked with a second generation family business. All siblings were involved hands on in working in the business. However, one of the siblings was regularly late to work, took long lunch breaks, did not attend meetings he was expected to and failed to reply to email communications. The rest of the family felt ashamed of his behaviour because it was obvious to employees and were not able to confront him with it for fear of having a scene in front of the rest of the employees in the company. They felt their trust in him had been betrayed and did not feel they could resort to addressing his performance with the support of the human resources department. This is because he was "an owner" and this would create a conflict with the employee that was confronting him in the HR department. His behaviour continued for a while until the morale of the company was being affected, particularly that of other colleagues in his department. Although the family trusted he was able to do the job, they were not able to address their concerns to improve matters for fear of being publicly shamed. During our work together they wanted to focus on improving their relationship as a family. They were able to regain the closeness they once had as siblings. In addition, they were also able to put his behaviour in the office into a broader perspective which enabled them to accept him as he was.

Financial Strains of the Business on the Family

The business may place great pressure on the owners and yet they may not be able to resolve the very aspect that would improve matters. I was requested to join in the work of a family who was greatly motivated and engaged in the process they had initiated with their advisor to resolve a specific matter related with the business. Time was of an essence and yet they found it very difficult to coordinate their diary. Every time they had to set up a new meeting they engaged in long conversations and debate, meetings being too far apart for the work to keep momentum. Difficulties in diary agreements had come to the point that the business was not running efficiently and tension begun to mount over time. Working with the family uncovered a deeply held belief in being busy as a sign of productivity, health and deserving of love and attention in the family. This belief came from the first generation family owners who worked very hard during the WWII. In their commitment to survive the war and support their country they adopted the practice of being busy and productive. This served them well and the family business prospered. They brought up the second generation with the belief that they should be busy and deserve the wealth they received from the first generation by their activity and good results. Parents were not going to spoil their children by just handing things over to them for no results.

Over time the second generation was even more successful than the first, each of them a champion in their chosen field of interest. The third generation came along and continued being driven, active and keen to succeed. They had been brought up as busy children, with many activities related to their education, sports and social engagements to promote the family's philanthropy. The result appeared to be that they were not able to truly make themselves available to others in the family. Having time would be like accepting that they were not busy enough, and therefore not deserving of what love they received from the family (in the concrete form of benefits or money). No one seemed to remember the war, as it had happened decades before; certainly they did not remember explicitly how the appearance of being busy connected with the family's history. Our work together helped them identify how the underlying belief in being busy was getting in the way of them making the time to meet their own needs for comfort, healing and relaxation as well as meeting the needs of the family to engage in the necessary changes for the survival of the business. Gradually unmasking this belief and replacing it with more up to date values and beliefs was essential for this family who was then able to develop cooperative problem solving skills to support each other. Gradually this had an impact on their diary and ability to be available to support each other constructively.

Conclusion

The field of family business is gaining greater attention as the difficulties of families involved in running a business together become more apparent. The work involved requires a long term perspective and an understanding of how to support families, how business operate and an explicit intention to address the relationship between the two with the family.

Families may not necessarily start their work requesting therapy for themselves, but rather start from a desire to address concrete behavioural goals. In time, families gain greater insight into their difficulties, requiring to renegotiate their work agreements with us and focus on the issues that may lie behind their initial request. This requires the use of sophisticated systemic family approaches over time and in cooperation with other family advisors.

Families involved in running their own business frequently face a world of paradoxes. Time, money, freedom to choose, happiness are a few paradoxes that appear to come up in multiple disguises. Time is a valued commodity and people who own their own business claim to own their time. This rarely translates into fewer obligations or less demands on their activity schedule. The paradox is that frequently owners find themselves busy: travelling, networking with others, problem solving, making important decisions, attending meetings with professionals who undertake the daily run of their investments, keeping up with what is happening in their enterprise or their competitor's. Although they own their time they are needed by others in order for the enterprise to prosper, as well as for the harmony of the family to flow. This means that families frequently face the dilemma of ranking complex interrelated priorities, rather than hold their diaries just to themselves.

Families are likely to understand the added value of an advisor that is trusted by all. In my experience, they can easily understand the importance of investing time to gain greater benefits by addressing the root of the problem affecting them, their business or the relationship between the two. I have found that the mindful use of principles derived from research and clinical practice in family systems are essential to the resolution of the paradoxes that these families face.

References

Kaye, K. (2010). *Trust in the family enterprise.* http://kaye.com/fambz/Trust2.pdf. sited 26 February 2019.

Rogers, C. (1951). *Client centered therapy: Its current practice, implications and theory.* London: Constable.

Strike, V. M. (2013). The most trusted advisor and the subtle advice process. *Family Firms Family Business Review, 26*(3), 293–313.

Editors' Reflections: The Way Forward

As we look back on the chapters in our text we are grateful to contributors for providing such a broad range of descriptions of long-term systemic applications and interventions. The chapters recount multiple stories of long-term systemic practice from settings as diverse as trauma work with individual adults, therapy across adolescent years, couple work in chronic illness, family/organisational interventions with family businesses as well as systemic supervision and support in the workplace and in ministry. We also note an unplanned, but engaging, diversity in the writing styles between the chapters, with some authors (Chimera, Draper and Vetere) drawing upon the voices of their clients to illuminate the journey of change, others (Houston, Sheehan and Vetere) focusing on the evolution of practitioner/client relational processes underpinning the same journey and yet others (Sheehan and Lang) drawing attention to the expansion of theoretical frameworks brought about by the long-term character of the work.

Yet, for all the richness of the preceding chapters, we are aware that the territory of long-term systemic psychotherapy is much larger than might be contained within the confines of this single set of chapters.

A. Vetere and J. Sheehan (eds.), *Long Term Systemic Therapy*,
Palgrave Texts in Counselling and Psychotherapy,
https://doi.org/10.1007/978-3-030-44511-9

For, example, the part played by culture within all the areas of long-term practice described within these pages needs careful exploration. Within the restaurant sector in the UK, for example, many immigrant groups of first, second and third generations run family businesses that bring together multicultural groups of staff with multicultural customer bases. In view of the make-up of these family businesses and their external environments, we wonder whether their assisting systemic consultants are required to address aspects of racism that either threaten the operation of internal organisational relationships or jeopardise the ongoing existence of such businesses through the effects of external environment permeated by racism. We might ask similar questions regarding culture and race in the contexts of long-term individual systemic psychotherapy or long-term systemic supervision. For example, how are differences with respect to culture and race managed within these relationships and how might the longevity character of such interventions impact upon the way such differences are experienced and managed within these relationships. The way forward must pay attention to these elements.

As editors we were also struck by the way all chapters in the volume made reference, either directly or indirectly, to attachment theory as a significant descriptive and explanatory framework underpinning long-term systemic interventions. Whether drawing upon this theory to account for the trauma-laden histories of many individuals or as a way of accounting for the healing quality of the long-term therapeutic relationship itself, these authors clearly see and experience attachment theory as a necessary perspective within the theoretical repertoires at the heart of their systemic practices.

Three of our chapters (Hanks, Lang, Sweeney and Daly) describe long-term systemic supervisory and support structures either within the workplace or with professional interest groups such as ministers or family therapists. We think the systemic training arena needs to know more about the prevalence of such long-term supervision structures as well as about the challenges and opportunities experienced by both supervisors and supervisees within them. The Hanks chapter provides us with an interesting and timely reminder that supervision was until relatively recently perceived as something that revealed weakness in practitioners receiving it. The idea of supervision as a time-limited remedy for deficits in novice or poorly functioning practitioners has slowly given way to a view of supervision as a multifaceted phenomenon with a multiplicity of functions, including the ongoing practice enrichment of highly skilled and experienced practitioners, operating across the whole professional life course.

The volume has also highlighted something important about the inter-linking of time and efficacy within the psychotherapy experience. Practitioners are accustomed to that familiar question often posed by clients within the first consultation: how long will it take to heal my affliction? While health insurance systems want to limit the number of therapeutic sessions clients receive for any problem or condition, the opening chapter (Vetere) reminds us that, from the perspective of the internal world of psychotherapy, the work takes as long as it takes. We are faced here by something profoundly counter-cultural about long-term systemic interventions which exist within larger cultural frameworks that privilege pre-packaged solutions and fixes that are valued for their speed of delivery.

Finally, it seems important to us that three of the chapter authors (Chimera, Draper and Vetere) included the voices of clients in their representations of long-term systemic psychotherapy. We see this as one small but important step on the journey towards making the experiences of clients an important reference point in the construction, theoretically and practically, of long-term systemic psychotherapy interventions. Along this journey we need research studies of different kinds to examine the efficacy of long-term systemic interventions as well to inform practitioners of those ingredients of long-term practice that clients associate most strongly with their progression along a path of recovery.

So, to conclude, we hope that you as interested readers, will be encouraged to speak and write about your experiences of long term systemic therapeutic work, supervision and consultation in its many forms and in its many practice contexts. As editors, we should be delighted to enter into correspondence and hope to see this topic have an 'airing' at systemic conferences.

Index

© The Editor(s) (if applicable) and The Author(s), under exclusive
license to Springer Nature Switzerland AG 2020
A. Vetere and J. Sheehan (eds.), *Long Term Systemic Therapy*,
Palgrave Texts in Counselling and Psychotherapy,
https://doi.org/10.1007/978-3-030-44511-9

Printed by Printforce, the Netherlands